# Dining In-Philadelphia

**A Collection of Gourmet Recipes for Complete
Meals from Philadelphia's Finest Restaurants**

Pearl Nipon

Foreword by Joan G. Hauser

**Peanut Butter Publishing**
Mercer Island, Washington

## TITLES IN SERIES

Feasting in Atlanta
Dining In–Baltimore
Dining In–Boston
Dining In–Chicago, Vol. I
Dining In–Chicago, Vol. II
Dining In–Dallas
Dining In–Denver
Dining In–Hawaii
Dining In–Houston, Vol. I
Dining In–Houston, Vol. II
Dining In–Kansas City
Dining In–Los Angeles
Dining In–Milwaukee
Dining In–Minneapolis/St. Paul
Dining In–Monterey Peninsula
Feasting In New Orleans
Dining In–Philadelphia
Dining In–Phoenix
Dining In–Pittsburgh
Dining In–Portland
Dining In–St. Louis
Dining In–San Francisco
Dining In–Seattle, Vol. II
Dining In–Sun Valley
Dining In–Washington, D.C.

Dining In–Toronto
Dining In–Vancouver, B.C.

Cover Photograph by Kenneth Redding
Illustrations by Neil Sweeney

ISBN 0-89716-039-8

## DEDICATION

This book, offering the finest culinary accomplishments of Philadelphia's finest restaurants, is dedicated to the Comprehensive Epilepsy Center of the Graduate Hospital in Philadelphia.

Through their efforts, they restore the joy of life (health) to children and adults affected by epilepsy. Their accomplishments will be furthered by proceeds from this book.

*Pearl Nipon*

# CONTENTS

# FOREWORD

**In** the last decade, Philadelphia has been the scene of a virtual explosion of new restaurants. Today the restaurant industry is one of the largest employers in the city, providing the discriminating diner with an abundance of choices. The emergence of many small restaurant "boutiques" specializing in innovative cuisine is a natural result of both local and national trends.

The renaissance of downtown Philadelphia—the renovation of Center City and the blossoming of Society Hill and the dock area—has brought the affluent and the young back to the city, providing a neighborhood clientele for the new restaurants. The ever-growing list of cultural events bring yet more people into the city in the evening. This sophisticated public demonstrates its respect for and appreciation of good food by its support of Philadelphia's excellent restaurants.

Nationally, a knowledge of sophisticated international cuisine is no longer the province of the elite. Concern about food and wine within and without the home has become a necessity for today's consumer. This is reflected in the ever-growing market for food and food-related products, from delicacy shops, to gourmet pots and pans, to enlightened dining in and out of the home.

Many of the young owners and chefs of Philadelphia's new restaurants reflect the crest of this new wave. Young and experimental, they have chosen to become restaurateurs because it represents a lifestyle they find desirable. As one said, "Owning my own restaurant allows me to be creative, to satisfy people, and to make a living—all on my own terms."

As many have discovered, the restaurant business is self-perpetuating. Although the cost of rents and overhead have grown appreciably, new restaurants continue to emerge. Philadelphia has become one of the premier restaurant centers in the country.

The restaurants included in this book are only a small number of those found in Philadelphia and its environs. In style of cuisine and price, the choices are immense, to the delight of residents and visitors to the "City of Brotherly Love."

Joan G. Hauser

# PREFACE

As a native Philadelphian, nothing has given me more pleasure than the resurgence of elegance and quality in metropolitan Phildelphia. Our marvelous restaurants are only one facet of the "new" Philadelphia enjoyed by my family and myself. The quality of life here allows us to enjoy country and city living with equal ease; it is delightful to have the best restaurants in America a mere twenty-five minutes from my doorstep.

As a sometime chef for my family and a long-time connoisseur of excellent cuisine, I was greatly impressed by the superb recipes so freely given by each chef. I also enjoyed receiving a private tour of so many creative kitchens. Most of all, I had fun experimenting on my own.

With the help of so many "trade secrets," I have added many delicious dishes to my repertoire. For me, to be elegantly gowned and superbly fêted is one of the greater pleasures of life. I hope that all my readers derive as much delight from this book as I did in its preparation.

*Pearl Nipon*

# ACKNOWLEDGMENTS

*I would like to thank Joan Siegel Straus, Joan G. Hauser, and her assistant, Michael Quinn, for their help in preparing this book.*

## Alouette

### Dinner for Six

Nouilles au Citron

Soupe Concombre Froide

Salade Verte Vinaigrette Gourmande

Fruits de Mer aux Petits Légumes

Poire Alouette

### Wines:

With the Nouilles—Ravel Vinho Verde
With the Fruits de Mer—Corton-Charlemagne

Kamol Phutlek and Cynthia Chiusa, Owners
Kamol Phutlek, Chef

Alouette's chef and co-owner, Kamol Phutlek, has studied at Paris's La Varenne cooking school, with Michel Guerard, and with the Troisgros brothers. He also brings to his knowledge of French cuisine many techniques learned in his native Thailand. He says, "To nouvelle cuisine I have brought distinctly Oriental touches, such as stir-frying, special seasonings, and methods of presentation. An example of one of my unique recipes would be chicken curry, which is accompanied by a rich cream sauce flavored with Thai curry-paste and fresh basil."

After working for many different restaurants, Kamol says, "I am delighted to be on my own at last, free to create the kinds of dishes I believe in. I strive always for freshness. I believe that all the ingredients should complement one another without losing their individual taste."

Kamol believes that presentation is an integral part of the preparation of his dishes. He says, "It is as important to please the eye as the palate." His own high standards lead him to supervise carefully the exact preparation of each dish that leaves his kitchen.

The atmosphere at Alouette complements Kamol's cuisine. The decor consists of exposed brick walls, a hardwood floor, quaint Victorian lamps, an antique sideboard, and a profusion of plants and flowers. His partner, Cynthia Chiusa, has chosen a setting that is simple and warmly inviting, encouraging patrons to relax and enjoy Kamol's food—the most important part of an evening at Alouette.

528 South Fifth Street

## NOUILLES AU CITRON

Olive oil
Salt
1 pound capellini noodles
3 tablespoons chopped fresh
    thyme
1 teaspoon finely chopped
    garlic

1 tablespoon lemon juice
Zest of 2 lemons, grated
Dash of Tabasco sauce
Ground black pepper
6 ounces prosciutto or baked
    ham, julienned

1. Bring a 5-quart pot of water to a boil. Add salt and a dash of olive oil, then the capellini. When the noodles are cooked al dente, drain in a colander and run under cold water. Place in a bowl and add a little olive oil to prevent sticking.
2. Add the thyme, garlic, lemon juice, zest, and Tabasco sauce to the cooked pasta and mix well. Season to taste with salt and pepper.
3. Sauté the ham in olive oil for 1 minute. Add the seasoned capellini to the pan and sauté until the pasta is hot. Check seasoning and adjust if necessary. Serve immediately.

*The pasta is most easily re-warmed in a teflon pan, for it has a tendency to stick. This dish can be served cold as well as hot. It is important to use only fresh herbs and to be sure that the pasta does not overcook.*

## SOUPE CONCOMBRE FROID

1½ pounds cucumbers, peeled
    and seeded
  3 tablespoons butter
  ¼ cup chopped onion
  ¼ cup chopped shallots
  6 cups chicken stock
  2 teaspoons white wine
    vinegar

¼ cup chopped fresh dill
¼ cup uncooked rice
   Heavy cream
   Salt and pepper
1 cup sour cream
1 tablespoon minced dill

1. Grate about 3 tablespoons cucumber and set aside. Cut the remainder into small pieces.
2. Slowly heat the butter in a skillet and sauté the onion and shallots until transparent. Add the cucumbers, chicken stock, vinegar, and dill. Bring to a boil and stir in the rice. Simmer partially covered for 25 minutes.
3. Purée the mixture in a blender. Thin with heavy cream if needed. Add salt and pepper to taste. Stir in ½ cup sour cream and allow soup to cool. Refrigerate.
4. Before serving, garnish each bowl of soup with 1 tablespoon sour cream, topped by grated cucumber and minced dill.

*This soup may also be served hot. However, be careful not to let it come to a boil after adding the cream.*

*Be sure to remove the dill stems before chopping.*

# ALOUETTE

## FRUITS DE MER AUX PETITS LÉGUMES

1½ pounds bay scallops
1½ pounds shrimp
6 ounces snow peas or julienned green beans
2 carrots, julienned
2 stalks celery, julienned
¼ pound plus 2 tablespoons butter
2 shallots, chopped

3 tablespoons fresh FINES HERBES
3 leeks, white part only, chopped
1 bunch scallions, julienned
Salt and pepper
1½ cups dry vermouth
Dash of lemon juice

1. Clean the scallops. Clean and devein the shrimp, leaving the tails on.
2. Clean the snow peas and cut off the ends.
3. Boil the julienned carrots for 2 minutes; remove from heat and run under cold water to stop the cooking.
4. Boil the celery and the green beans, if used, for 1 minute; run under cold water. If using snow peas, boil separately for 15 seconds and run under cold water.
5. Heat 4 tablespoons butter in a large sauté pan. Add the shallots and sauté for 1 minute. Add the shrimp, then the bay scallops. When the shrimp turn slightly pink, after 2 or 3 minutes, add the Fines Herbes. Add the remaining vegetables, salt and pepper, and wine. Add the remaining butter in small dots. Bring to a boil.
6. Remove the vegetables and shellfish with a slotted spoon. Set aside and keep warm. Reduce the sauce by half and add a dash of lemon juice. Check the seasoning and adjust if necessary. Pour the sauce over the vegetables and shellfish and serve.

### FINES HERBES

Chopped tarragon
Chopped chives

Chopped parsley
Chopped lemon thyme

Use equal amounts of each ingredient.

*This is a very colorful entrée and a favorite among our customers.*

## SALADE VERTE VINAIGRETTE GOURMANDE

1  *large head red leaf lettuce*          *DRESSING*
1  *bunch watercress*

Toss the greens and combine with Dressing.

### *DRESSING*

1  *tablespoon lemon juice*         1  *tablespoon vinegar*
   *Salt and pepper*                   1  *tablespoon chopped chives*
2  *tablespoons olive oil*          1  *tablespoon chopped*
2  *tablespoons vegetable oil*         *tarragon*

In a bowl, mix together the lemon juice, salt, and pepper. Add the olive oil and vegetable oil. Add the vinegar, chives, and tarragon. Whisk well.

*Again, I repeat the importance of using fresh herbs and spices. I have an herb and spice garden at the restaurant which I find invaluable. The salad dressing may be prepared several hours in advance and refrigerated.*

## POIRE ALOUETTE

6  *medium-size Bartlett pears*        1  *vanilla bean*
¼  *cup lemon juice*                *RASPBERRY SAUCE*
1 to 1½  *quarts white wine*          *CRÈME FRAÎCHE*
2  *cups sugar*                   *Mint leaves*

1. Cut off the bottoms of the pears so that they will stand up. Peel off the skins, leaving the stems, and remove the cores. Rub the pears with lemon juice, or soak in a mixture of water and lemon juice, so that they will not discolor while standing.
2. Bring the wine, sugar, and vanilla to a boil. Add the pears and cover. When the wine returns to a boil, turn the heat down and simmer 10 to 15 minutes, or until the pears are soft. Be careful that the pears do not overcook. Remove from heat and let cool. Refrigerate until needed.

3. Pour 2 tablespoons Raspberry Sauce onto each plate. Fill a pastry bag with Crème Fraîche, attaching a very small tip. Beginning in the center, make an open spiral around each plate. Draw gently with a knife tip as though slicing a pie though not so deep, to draw the lines to create a scalloped design.
4. Drain the pears and insert one in the center of each plate. Put fresh mint leaves near stem of each pear. Serve.

### *RASPBERRY SAUCE*

½ *pound fresh or frozen raspberries*
½ *cup sugar*

*Dash of lemon juice*
1 *tablespoon Grand Marnier*

Purée the raspberries in a blender. Add the sugar and purée again. Strain through a fine sieve. Add the lemon juice and Grand Marnier. Chill.

### *CRÈME FRAÎCHE*

1 *cup buttermilk, sour cream, or yogurt*

2 *cups heavy cream*

1. In a saucepan, heat the buttermilk and heavy cream until it reaches body temperature.
2. Pour into a container and partially cover. Allow to stand for 6 to 8 hours at room temperature, when it will become thickened and slightly acid in taste. Then stir, cover, and refrigerate.

*The mixture may be kept for as long as one week. When preparing a new mixture of crème fraîche, the old crème fraîche may be used as a substitute for buttermilk, sour cream, or yogurt.*

*When we serve Poire Alouette, many customers remark that it is too pretty to eat. But I've yet to see one left unfinished on the dessert plate.*

**Le Bec-Fin**

Dinner for Four

Salade de Fruits de Mer

Poulet au Vinaigre de Vin et Gousses d'Ail

Gratin des Capucins

Pommes Boulangère

Chocolate Soufflé

Wine:

Meursault, 1978

Georges Perrier, Proprietor and Chef

Jean-Pierre Tardy, Chef

## LE BEC-FIN

**Le** Bec-Fin, a monument to the re-creation of traditional French cuisine, was opened by Georges Perrier in 1969. M. Perrier, who trained at Beaumariène and worked under Chef Point at La Pyramide in Vienne, says, "To me, it is essential to maintain the tradition and integrity of great cuisine. Every province in France has its own cuisine. If that is lost, we lose the basis upon which we are able to create.

"Today," he continues, "many chefs own their own restaurants. This allows them the freedom to be innovative and has led in the last half century to a gradual evolution in cooking. Nouvelle cuisine, far from being something new, is merely an extreme modification of traditional cooking. Personally, I do not believe it is wise to go too far from our roots."

M. Perrier, who has been cooking for twenty-seven years, is a Maître Cuisinier and Chef d'Honneur, international titles given to very few chefs in the world. "Yet," he says, "I feel I have just started to really cook after all that time. Each dish that I make reflects my mood and the inspiration of the moment. To me, cooking is a complete and total art form."

He finds cooking in America challenging and fulfilling. "The American palate has become one of great sophistication. Fortunately, I now find that I can purchase all the ingredients I need for my cooking here in America, which was not always true in the past. In many cases, I have developed my own sources of supply by encouraging the production of the essential fresh ingredients I need."

The decor at Le Bec-Fin is Louis the Sixteenth. Its traditional and classical opulence is enhanced by the fine table settings. "Beautiful decor and excellent service are important," says M. Perrier. "I have designed Le Bec-Fin to make my patrons feel as if they are my guests in my home. Yet I never forget that they are paying for excellent cuisine. Only superb food can create a superb restaurant."

Long considered the doyen of Philadelphia restaurants, Le Bec-Fin offers each guest, if only for a night, the opportunity to revel in the baroque splendor of magnificent food in a magnificent setting.

1312 Spruce Street

# LE BEC-FIN

## SALADE DE FRUITS DE MER

3 heads Bibb lettuce
4 ounces salmon, julienned
1 pound bay scallops,
  coarsley chopped
2 tablespoons butter
  Salt and pepper to taste

1 ounce cognac
1 cup baby shrimp
1 teaspoon finely chopped
  fresh chives or tarragon
DRESSING

1. Wash and dry lettuce. Arrange on individual salad plates. Divide salmon over each plate.
2. Sauté bay scallops in 1 tablespoon butter over medium flame for 1 minute, adding salt and pepper to taste. Flambé with cognac. Spoon out scallops and drain on paper towels. Reserve liquid and add it to the Dressing.
3. Sauté baby shrimp in remaining butter over medium flame for 1 minute. Drain on paper towels. Reserve 1 tablespoon of shrimp liquid for Dressing.
4. Divide hot shrimp and scallops onto each lettuce bed. Sprinkle with chives or tarragon. Spoon Dressing over each plate. Serve.

### DRESSING

1 teaspoon Dijon mustard
1 to 2 teaspoons sherry vinegar
  Salt and pepper
1 tablespoon reserved
  shrimp liquid

1 tablespoon reserved
  scallop liquid
¾ cup olive oil

1. Whisk mustard, sherry vinegar, salt and pepper together. Add scallop and shrimp liquids.
2. Add olive oil gradually and whisk again briskly.

*I came up with this recipe for use on a television program because it is simple and easily demonstrated on camera. I like the contrast between the warm shellfish and the cool salad and dressing. This should be served immediately after preparation.*

# LE BEC-FIN

## POULET AU VINAIGRE DE VIN ET GOUSSES D'AIL

*You may add 1 teaspoon of chopped parsley or 1 teaspoon of chopped chives.
Red wine vinegar may be substituted for sherry vinegar.*

| | |
|---|---|
| 4 cornish hens (6 to 8-ounces each) | 2 bay leaves |
| Salt and pepper | 15 cloves garlic, unpeeled |
| 2 tablespoons butter | 2½ ounces sherry vinegar |
| 1 tablespoon vegetable oil | 4 cups chicken broth |
| ½ bunch parsley | 3 tomatoes, peeled, seeded, and chopped |
| Pinch of thyme | 1 tablespoon tomato paste |

1. Salt and pepper hens.
2. Heat 1 tablespoon butter and oil in a pot. Sauté hens, browning on both sides. Make a bouquet garni by tying together parsley, thyme and bay leaves in cheesecloth. When hens are brown, add garlic and bouquet garni. Cover pot and cook on low flame for 20 minutes. Remove grease from pot. Add vinegar, chicken broth, half of the tomatoes, and the tomato paste. Cook for 15 minutes, covered, over a low flame.
3. Remove chicken and put aside, keeping it warm.
4. Remove bouquet garni and reduce sauce until it coats the back of a spoon by turning up heat and cooking, uncovered, for about 5 minutes. If the sauce is too liquid, add arrowroot or cornstarch. Press sauce through a strainer onto remaining tomato. Return to pot, season, add remaining butter, and simmer for 5 minutes.
5. To serve, hens may be quartered or served whole as you prefer. Serve the sauce on the side.

*This recipe, with a subtle flavor of garlic, is my own. It is neither too light nor too heavy.*

### GRATIN DES CAPUCINS

*This dish is based on a traditional* Haut Savoie *recipe, but, as always, I relied on the inspiration of the moment to make it uniquely mine. The noisette brings out the flavor of the spinach.*

| | |
|---|---|
| 5 tablespoons butter | 1½ cups heavy cream |
| 1 pound mushrooms, cleaned and sliced | 6 to 8 artichoke bottoms |
| Salt and pepper | 2 bunches fresh spinach, cooked and chopped |

1. Melt 2 tablespoons butter in a copper pan. Add mushrooms and salt and pepper to taste. Cook for 5 minutes. Cover with 1 cup heavy cream and reduce to thicken sauce.
2. Slice artichoke bottoms and sauté in small pan for 2 minutes in 1 tablespoon butter, adding salt and pepper to taste.
3. Create a butter noisette by browning 2 tablespoons butter in a sauté pan. Add the cooked and chopped spinach, salt, and pepper. Sauté, agitating the pan until spinach is heated through.
4. Spread cooked spinach to cover the bottom of a copper au gratin serving dish. Place the sautéed artichokes on top of spinach to form another layer. Add the cooked mushrooms to the top. Add remaining heavy cream.
5. Cook in a bain-marie in a 350° oven for 10 to 15 minutes, or until lightly browned on top. Serve.

*This dish may be prepared ahead of time. If so, be sure to add enough extra cream before baking to keep it moist.*

### POMMES BOULANGÈRE

4 to 6 large Idaho potatoes
2 tablespoons butter
2 tablespoons oil
   Salt and pepper
   Pinch of thyme

½ bay leaf, crumbled
½ pound bacon, thinly sliced
1 medium onion, sliced
1½ cups chicken stock

*If necessary, the potatoes may be sliced ahead of time. If so, be sure to keep them in cold water; drain and dry them thoroughly before use.*

1. Slice the potatoes on a mandolin slicer so that they are ⅛″ thick. In a large sauté pan, heat 1 tablespoon butter and 2 tablespoons oil. Lightly sauté potato slices with salt and pepper, thyme, and crumbled bay leaf for 10 minutes, turning frequently until golden brown.
2. Meanwhile, in a separate pan, cook bacon for 2 minutes on each side over medium heat. Drain off fat and place bacon on paper toweling to absorb the excess fat.
3. Sauté onion in 1 tablespoon butter in a separate pan over medium heat for 5 minutes or until golden brown.
4. Put potatoes, onion, and bacon in a gratin serving dish and mix. Add enough chicken stock to nearly cover potatoes. Bring to boil on top of the stove.
5. Remove from stove top and put in a 350° oven for 15 minutes, or until golden brown. Serve.

*If there is too much stock in pot after baking, put pot on top of stove and reduce.*

### CHOCOLATE SOUFFLÉ

¾ pound semisweet
   chocolate
1¼ cups milk
  9 eggs, separated

1 cup sugar
3¼ cups heavy cream
½ cup whipped cream
   for decoration

1. Melt the chocolate with milk in a heavy pot. Remove from heat
2. Put ¼ cup sugar and the egg yolks into a mixing bowl and beat for 2 minutes. Add the melted chocolate and continue to beat until well mixed. Transfer mixture to a larger bowl.
3. Put heavy cream in original mixing bowl and beat until it reaches the consistency of a thick sauce. Add cream to larger bowl containing chocolate and beat in.
4. Put ¾ cup sugar and ½ cup water in a heavy saucepan and bring to the soft ball (234° to 240°) stage. As the mixture starts to boil, paint the sides of the pan with a pastry brush dipped in water to cleanse away impurities in the sugar.
5. Meanwhile, beat the egg whites until they form soft peaks. Add the simple syrup mixture and beat for 5 minutes. Add to chocolate, whisking well.
6. Pour into a (6-cup) soufflé dish with a high aluminum collar and freeze for 24 hours. Decorate with whipped cream and serve in wedges.

*Everyone likes chocolate so much that this is a perfect ending to a meal.*

*Dinner for Six*

*Carpaccio*

*Beefsteak Tomato Salad*

*Veal Casablanca*

*Roast Potatoes*

*Sautéed String Beans*

*Bananas à la Moyer*

*Café Sorcerer*

*Wines:*

*Pinot Grìgio, Livio Felluga, 1978*

*Callaway Dry Chenin Blanc, 1979*

*Mrs. Bernard J. Kravitz and Eli Karetny, Propietors*
*Lewis Norsworthy, General Manager*
*Pat Duffey, Chef*

**B**ogart's, located in the Hotel Latham, has an ambiance all its own. Modeled after Rick's Bar, from Humphrey Bogart's *Casablanca* period, the atmosphere is both sophisticated and intimate. From the small bar to the Casablanca café decor, the guest feels that he has wandered into a very special private club. Its manager, Lewis Norsworthy, is aware of the importance of mood. He says, "Restaurants must be creative. With the many excellent restaurants we have here in Philadelpia, nothing can be taken for granted any more."

Bogart's takes pride in its long list of regular clientele. Lewis says, "I am on a first-name basis with many of our patrons. They know the waiters as well and feel as comfortable dining here as they do at home."

Pat Duffey, the chef, trained at Paris's La Varenne school. Her specialty is Northern Italian cuisine, but she describes Bogart's menu as "diverse international cuisine." She says, "It's a real challenge. We are open seven days a week, three meals a day. We must satisfy those of our clients who prefer simple prime ribs as well as those who have more sophisticated taste. We add unusual touches to all of our dishes and become most venturesome with our daily gourmet creations."

A specialty at Bogart's is tableside cooking. Many dishes are prepared, with great panache, in front of the diner. "This," Lewis says, "adds an element of drama to our food presentation. It also gives our guest a feeling of participation in the meal they are about to have."

For an understated version of the classic bistro and an interesting dining experience, Bogart's is a convenient and pleasantly inviting club to join.

**17th and Walnut Streets**

## CARPACCIO

*The filet should be nearly frozen to facilitate slicing.*

| | |
|---|---|
| 1½ cups heavy cream | Salt and pepper |
| 3 ounces shallots, chopped | 1½ pounds filet mignon, |
| 3 ounces fresh, grated | sliced very thin |
| horseradish | Watercress sprigs |
| 1½ ounces fresh, chopped | Lemon wedges |
| parsley | |

1. Whip heavy cream until stiff. Fold in the shallots, horseradish, and parsley. Add salt and pepper to taste.
2. Place a dollop of whipped cream in the center of each filet slice and roll up. Place on a chilled plate and garnish with watercress and lemon slices.

*It is essential to use fresh herbs for this recipe, our version of steak tartare.*

## BEEFSTEAK TOMATO SALAD

| | |
|---|---|
| 6 romaine leaves | 12 anchovy fillets |
| 6 large New Jersey beefsteak | VINAIGRETTE DRESSING |
| tomatoes | (see next page) |
| 1½ Bermuda onions, chopped | Parsley, coarsely chopped |

1. Place cleaned romaine leaves on chilled salad plates.
2. Cut tomatoes in quarters without cutting all the way through. Fan out the sides so that it creates a large rosette. Set onto romaine.
3. Stuff center of each tomato with chopped onion. Place 2 anchovy fillets in an "x" across the top.
4. Ladle Vinaigrette over each plate. Sprinkle parsley on top for garnish. Serve.

# BOGART'S

### VINAIGRETTE DRESSING

⅓ cup red wine vinegar
1½ teaspoons Dijon mustard
1 ounce chopped shallots

Salt and pepper
1 cup vegetable oil

Combine first 4 ingredients in a small bowl. Whisk in oil in a stream, beating until well blended.

*The presentation of this salad is colorful and unusual, with the contrast of the red tomatoes, the green lettuce, the white onions, and the "x" created by the anchovies.*

## VEAL CASABLANCA

18 (1½-ounce) medallions
    of veal, trimmed from
    leg and flattened
    Salt and pepper
¾ cup flour
3 tablespoons butter
8 ounces mushrooms, sliced
8 ounces tomato, peeled,
    seeded, and julienned

1 ounce shallots, chopped
5 ounces chablis
2 lemons, juiced
1 cup heavy cream
1 ounce caviar
    Chopped parsley

1. Season veal with salt and pepper. Dredge in flour.
2. In a heated sauté pan, melt butter and add veal. Brown lightly for 1 minute on both sides. Remove from pan and keep warm.
3. Add mushrooms, tomatoes, and shallots to pan. Sauté lightly for 2 minutes. Deglaze pan with wine and reduce by half over high heat. Add lemon juice. Stir in heavy cream and reduce until slightly thickened. Check seasoning. Return veal to pan and heat for 2 minutes.
4. To serve, place 3 pieces of veal on each plate and top with sauce. Sprinkle each with caviar and chopped parsley before serving.

*This surprisingly hearty dish combines the elegance of caviar with the luxury of a rich cream sauce.*

## OVEN ROASTED POTATOES

6  large Idaho potatoes,
    peeled and cut into 1"
    cubes
3  ounces vegetable oil
1  teaspoon salt
1  teaspoon pepper

½  teaspoon rosemary
3  cloves garlic, finely
    chopped
2  tablespoons chopped
    parsley

1. Preheat oven to 400°.
2. Put vegetable oil in the bottom of a 9" × 12" roasting pan and set on stove, allowing oil to become very hot. Add potatoes to pan and leave on top of flame for a few minutes, shaking pan rapidly several times.
3. Set pan into preheated oven for 20 minutes. Add salt, pepper, rosemary, and garlic and cook for 10 more minutes. Serve garnished with chopped parsley.

*The garlic and rosemary enhance the natural flavor of the potato in this crisply textured dish.*

## SAUTÉED STRING BEANS

½  pound young string beans
6  tablespoons butter

4  shallots, chopped
    Salt and pepper to taste

1. Snap the ends off of the string beans. Blanch in rapidly boiling water for 7 or 8 minutes, or until crisp and tender.
2. Melt butter in sauté pan. Add string beans, chopped shallots, salt and pepper. Sauté for approximately 5 minutes and serve.

### BANANAS A LA MOYER

6 tablespoons sweet butter
6 tablespoons light brown sugar
6 bananas, sliced
2 pinches of cinnamon

¾ ounce banana liqueur
1½ ounces dark rum
2 dashes Kahlua
1½ quarts vanilla ice cream
⅓ cup sliced, toasted almonds

1. Melt butter in pan. Add brown sugar. When sugar has melted, add bananas to the pan with cinnamon.
2. Flame in pan with banana liqueur. Flame again with rum. Add Kahlua.
3. Serve over vanilla ice cream in coupe glasses. Sprinkle with almonds.

*This is typical of our table-side dishes. The effect is dashing and dramatic.*

## CAFÉ SORCERER

½ lemon             1 teaspoon cinnamon
¼ cup sugar        48 ounces coffee
7½ ounces Frangelico    1 cup whipped cream
3 ounces Amaretto

1. Using 12-ounce heat-proof glasses, rim the edge of each glass with a lemon twist. Dip the rims in a saucer of sugar.
2. Caramelize the rim of each glass over a flame. When the glass is warm, add 1¼ ounces Frangelico and ½ ounce Amaretto. Continue to heat by tipping glass so that liqueur barely touches rim until the liqueur flames.
3. Sprinkle ¼ teaspoon of cinnamon into each glass. Add coffee and divide whipped cream among glasses. Sprinkle a little cinnamon on top. Serve.

*The cinnamon creates a sparkling effect, which is the origin of the name "sorcerer".*

# BOOKBINDER'S

*Dinner for Four*

*Oysters à la Bookbinder*

*Clam Chowder*

*Lobster Stuffed with Crabmeat*

*Stuffed Baked Potato*

*Stewed Tomatoes*

*Rice Pudding*

*Albert Taxin, Owner*

*Nathaniel Frison, Chef*

**B**ookbinder's is a Philadelphia classic, first opened in 1865. For nearly forty years it has been owned by the Taxin family. Its specialty is fresh seafood, and its location near the docks was designed to allow the original owner to purchase his supplies right off the ships as they docked. Today, the Taxins demand the same freshness in the food they serve. Albert Taxin describes his father John as "still picking up his own home-grown vegetables for the restaurant all summer in his chauffeur-driven limousine."

Albert Taxin considers the restaurant as "definitely a family affair." He says, "I grew up in the restaurant. It's the way our family relaxes." Many of the large staff at Bookbinder's are part of the Bookbinder "family." Chef Nathaniel Frison has been with the restaurant for forty-two years, beginning as a kitchen man and is now described by Albert Taxin as "the best chef in Philadelphia."

The decor is eclectic. Each of the restaurant's many rooms has a different ambiance and all reek with history. The Taxins are collectors—from ancient firearms to presidential memorabilia, Currier and Ives prints, old playbills, and pictures of the many celebrities and presidents who have visited Bookbinder's. Wandering through the restaurant, the diner's eye is caught by a fascinating profusion of anecdotal historical *objets*.

Bookbinder's is a relaxed, cheerful, and bountiful place to eat. Albert Taxin says, "The key to our success is simplicity. We serve ample portions of traditional American food, simply prepared, yet with the best and freshest ingredients." As a Philadelphia institution, Bookbinder's has maintained a sense of its own history as well as the "old-fashioned" quality of its food.

125 Walnut Street

## OYSTERS A LA BOOKBINDER

*This recipe may be made with more oysters, depending upon the rest of the dinner planned. It may also be served as a main course.*

| | |
|---|---|
| 12 oysters | ½ cup warm milk |
| 1 large mushroom, finely chopped | ¼ cup cooked oatmeal<br>Salt and pepper |
| 1 teaspoon minced onion | 1 tablespoon minced parsley |
| 3 tablespoons butter | 3 tablespoons grated |
| 1 teaspoon flour | Parmesan cheese |

1. Wash and shuck oysters, putting them on the half shell.
2. Sauté the mushroom and onion in 1 tablespoon butter until soft but not browned. Add flour and stir to blend. Add the milk and stir until thickened. Add the oatmeal and stir well. Season to taste with salt and pepper. Stir in the parsley.
3. Place the oysters under the broiler for 4 minutes. Remove and cover each oyster with some sauce. Sprinkle with Parmesan cheese. Melt 2 tablespoons butter and drizzle a few drops over oysters. Return to broiler and cook for 5 minutes or until browned.

## BOOKBINDER'S

### CLAM CHOWDER

*This is an original Bookbinder's recipe. It may be kept for a week. The clam base may be purchased at any fish market.*

2 cups large clams (about 8 clams)
2 large potatoes, diced
2 medium-size onions, sliced
2 bell peppers, finely chopped
2 stalks celery, finely chopped

1 tablespoon paprika
2 tablespoons butter
2 tablespoons flour
1 tablespoon Accent
1 quart clam stock
2 tablespoons clam base
1 (12-ounce) can whole tomatoes, chopped and drained

1. Steam the clams in 1 quart of water in a large kettle. Reserve liquid to use as clam stock. Dice the clams.
2. Cook the potatoes separately in 2 cups of boiling water for 5 to 10 minutes. Drain.
3. In a large pot, sauté the onion, peppers, celery, and paprika in butter until the vegetables are tender, about 6 minutes. Add the flour and Accent, stirring well so that the mixture does not brown. Add the clam stock, clam base, potatoes, and clams. Allow to simmer for 15 minutes.
4. Add the tomatoes and simmer for 5 to 10 minutes, covered. Serve.

## LOBSTER STUFFED WITH CRABMEAT

4 (1¼-pound) lobsters
4 tablespoons melted butter
Dash of paprika

CRABMEAT STUFFING
Lemon, parsley and
watercress

1. Put each live lobster on its back and split down the middle with a cleaver, being careful not to cut through the back shell. Remove sand bag near the middle of the head. Crack claws with a knife to let water out.
2. Baste lobster with melted butter and paprika, soaking thoroughly. Broil 3" from heat for 15 to 20 minutes until lightly browned.
3. Put warm stuffing on top of lobster meat, just as you would apply frosting to a cake. Brown again under the broiler for 2 to 3 minutes.
4. To serve, garnish with lemon, parsley and watercress. Provide melted butter on the side.

*This unique recipe must be made with live lobsters. Lobsters may be kept in the refrigerator for eight hours. Never put them in fresh water.*

### CRABMEAT STUFFING

¼ cup butter
¼ cup flour
1 cup milk
  Salt and pepper
¼ cup diced green pepper
2 pimientos, diced

½ tablespoon Worcestershire
  sauce
2 tablespoons minced
  parsley
2 pounds crabmeat
2 egg yolks, well beaten

1. In a large sauté pan over medium heat, melt the butter, add the flour, and stir until smooth. Add the milk and continue cooking, stirring constantly, until thickened.
2. Add the remaining ingredients and mix well. Continue cooking until heated through, but do not allow to boil.

### STUFFED BAKED POTATOES

*This country-style vegetable is an old-fashioned American recipe.*

4 large Idaho baking
 potatoes
4 tablespoons sour cream
2 tablespoons chopped chives

7 tablespoons grated Swiss
 or American cheese
Paprika

1.  Bake potatoes at 350° for 1 hour, or until thoroughly done.
2.  Cut each potato in half vertically. Remove potatoes from the skin, being careful not to damage the skin.
3.  Place potatoes in bowl with sour cream and mash. Add chopped chives and 3 tablespoons of cheese. Replace filling in skins. Sprinkle with remaining grated cheese and paprika.
4.  Brown under broiler until cheese melts. Serve.

### STEWED TOMATOES

1 (16-ounce) can whole
 tomatoes
½ tablespoon butter
½ teaspoon salt

½ teaspoon sugar
1 tablespoon cornstarch
1 tablespoon diced celery
1 tablespoon diced onion

Bring all ingredients to a boil; reduce heat and simmer for 10 minutes or until mixture is of medium thickness.

## BOOKBINDER'S

### RICE PUDDING

| | |
|---|---|
| 1 cup uncooked rice | ¼ teaspoon cinnamon |
| 1½ quarts milk | ¾ cup sugar |
| 1 teaspoon salt | 1 egg, well beaten |
| ¼ teaspoon nutmeg | 2 tablespoons butter, |
| 1½ teaspoons vanilla | melted |

1. Place the milk, salt, and rice in a saucepan. Bring to a slow boil and cook uncovered over low heat for 20 minutes.
2. Season with nutmeg, vanilla, cinnamon, and sugar. Add the egg and butter and mix well.
3. Pour into a baking dish and brown lightly under the broiler, watching carefully, for 1 minute. Allow to cool and chill thoroughly before serving.

*This traditional dessert may be kept a week in the refrigerator. The tricky part of this recipe is the addition of the egg. Be sure that it is extremely well beaten and stir constantly as you add it to the pudding.*

# LA CAMARGUE

*Dinner for Six*

*Potage Germiny*

*Coquilles aux Poireaux*

*Veau Vaccarès*

*Salade Marcel*

*Mocha Walnut Meringue*

*Wine:*

*a Sancerre, or*
*Gigondas, Cuvée du Président*

*Marcel Brosette, Proprietor and Chef*
*Peter Leary, Pastry Chef*

# LA CAMARGUE

**To** enter La Camargue is to step into a small French country inn. Marcel Brosette, its owner and chef, says, "I have tried to keep the flavor of my former home. La Camargue is a province in the south of France. It is the home of wild horses and pink flamingos; it is there that most of the bulls used in Spanish rings are bred. The Gypsies come to Vaccarès every year for their annual festival."

Marcel trained at Annecy, Lyons, and Switzerland. In Lyons, he worked at Hotel Sofitel under Chef Marc Alix, whom he considers one of the best chefs in the world. In Philadelphia, he worked with Georges Perrier at Le Bec-Fin for three years before opening La Camargue six years ago. "Like a typical Frenchman," he says, "I have a great desire to be independent. At La Camargue, I have the freedom to make my own decisions and express my personal taste."

Marcel describes his cuisine as "classic French with a little joi de vivre, touches from Lyons and Vaccarès." He adds, "Ideally, one should buy fresh produce each morning in the market, cook it without losing or overpowering the taste, and serve it the same day as soon as it is cooked. The freshness of all ingredients is essential.

"At La Camargue, we serve food of the same quality as other more formal restaurants, but we do it in a relaxed manner. We don't want to be only a special occasion place. Our guests enjoy our food and atmosphere without feeling they must make a whole evening of it. One thing I always try to do is to greet each guest personally so they will feel welcomed and at home."

Bull horns hang over the huge fireplace at La Camargue. Each evening, a classical guitarist plays for Marcel's guests as they enjoy Tapenade, a typical hors d'oeuvre from southern France, with their drinks. Fresh flowers appear on each table; the waiters and waitresses wear the traditional black and white French uniforms. A relaxed setting and a formal meal are the successful combination that appeals to the discriminating diner, whether a "regular" or a new guest.

1119 Walnut Street

## *LA CAMARGUE*

### POTAGE GERMINY

2  ounces fresh sorrel
1  tablespoon butter
6  cups beef or chicken
   consommé

6  egg yolks
1  cup heavy cream
   Salt and pepper

1. Carefully wash sorrel and cook slowly in butter for 5 minutes.
2. In another pot, bring consommé to a boil.
3. In a bowl, combine yolks and cream, whisking until thoroughly blended. Continue whisking and slowly pour boiling consommé onto the cream/yolk mixture. Return to heat and cook slowly until mixture thickens. Add cooked sorrel and season with salt and pepper to taste.

*This soup must not boil or the egg yolks will curdle. This old classic recipe dates from a time when there were fifty cooks in the kitchen. It must be finished at the last moment and served immediately.*

## COQUILLES AUX POIREAUX

| | |
|---|---|
| 1½ pounds bay scallops | 3 tablespoons butter |
| 1 large or 2 small leeks, white part only, finely julienned | ⅓ cup Ricard |
| | 1½ cups heavy cream |
| | Salt and pepper |

1. Sauté scallops and leeks in butter over high heat until scallops are cooked, but still tender. Deglaze pan with Ricard. Remove scallops to a warm plate.
2. Add heavy cream to pan and boil slowly for approximately 5 minutes or until sauce has reduced to a light coating consistency.
3. Replace scallops in pan and season with salt and pepper. Serve.

*Scallops must not be allowed to boil in the sauce or they will toughen. The freshest scallops possible must be used. This northeastern French recipe is very similar to nouvelle cuisine in that it demands fresh ingredients and utilizes a minimum of cooking time.*

*Ricard is a very popular French licorice-flavored apéritif.*

# LA CAMARGUE

## VEAU VACCARÈS

12 (3-ounce) veal medallions
¼ cup flour
3 tablespoons butter
2 large or 3 small green peppers, seeded and cut into a fine julienne
¼ pound imported ham, julienned

¼ pound mushrooms, cleaned and thinly sliced
⅓ cup Madeira
3½ cups VEAL STOCK (see next page)
1½ cups green olives, pitted and sliced
Salt and pepper

1. Lightly flour medallions and sauté in butter until tender, or about 2 minutes on each side. Remove veal to a warm plate.
2. Without cleaning pan, sauté the peppers for 2 minutes. Add ham and mushrooms and sauté for an additional minute. Add the Madeira and Veal Stock. Boil slowly until the sauce thickens to coat the back of a spoon, about 20 minutes. Add olives and salt and pepper to taste.
3. To serve, put 2 medallions on each plate and cover with the sauce.

*Season this original dish carefully, as the ham and olives vary greatly in saltiness.*

*Be sure to remove any white ribs from the inside of the green peppers as this will make them taste bitter. The best quality of veal should be used.*

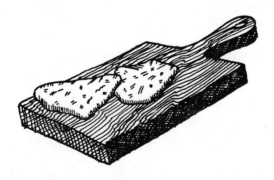

## VEAL STOCK

*This recipe yields 2 to 3 quarts and can be stored in the refrigerator for 2 weeks to be used for other dishes.*

| | |
|---|---|
| 3 pounds lean raw veal shank meat | 2 onions, peeled |
| 4 pounds raw veal bones, cracked | 2 stalks celery |
| | 2 leeks (optional) |
| 2 carrots, scraped | BOUQUET GARNI |
| | 2 teaspoons salt |

1. Place the meat and bones in a kettle. Cover with cold water, bring to the boil and boil slowly for 5 minutes. Drain, and rinse the bones and meat under cold water to remove all scum. Rinse the kettle clean.
2. Place the bones and meat back into the kettle, cover with cold water, bring to a simmer, and skim as necessary. Then add the vegetables, herbs, and seasonings. Simmer the stock for 4 to 5 hours.
3. Strain through a fine sieve or muslin.

*Veal stock is simple but takes time; the flavor is worth the effort.*

## BOUQUET GARNI

| | |
|---|---|
| ¼ teaspoon thyme | 2 unpeeled garlic cloves |
| 1 bay leaf | 2 whole cloves |
| 6 parsley sprigs | |

Tie all ingredients together in a washed cheesecloth.

## SALADE MARCEL

3 endives
1 bunch fresh watercress
1 small head Bibb lettuce
2 large or 3 small crisp and flavorful apples

1½ cups freshly shelled walnuts
VINAIGRETTE DRESSING
6 small wedges Brie cheese

1. Wash, core, and slice endive. Wash watercress and remove stems. Wash lettuce and tear into bite-size pieces. Peel, core, and slice apples into small wedges.
2. Combine washed and dried greens in a large bowl. Add apple wedges, walnuts, and enough Vinaigrette Dressing to just coat contents of bowl. Toss lightly to mix.
3. Serve on cold salad plates. Top each salad with a wedge of Brie.

*The Brie must be very soft, ripe, and runny.*

### VINAIGRETTE DRESSING

1 egg yolk
2 tablespoons wine vinegar
1 tablespoon Dijon mustard

1 cup high-quality salad oil
Salt and pepper

Combine and blend egg yolk, vinegar, and mustard. Whisk in oil slowly until oil is absorbed. Season to taste.

# LA CAMARGUE

## MOCHA WALNUT MERINGUE

1 cup granulated sugar
1 cup finely ground walnuts
1 cup egg whites, at room
  temperature
  Pinch of salt
½ teaspoon cream of tartar
2 pounds sweet butter, at
  room temperature
1 pound powdered sugar,
  sifted

3 egg yolks, beaten
4 tablespoons heavy cream
1 tablespoon warmed Kahlua
2 tablespoons instant coffee
  powder
½ cup chopped walnuts,
  for garnish
  Powdered sugar, for
  garnish

1. Preheat oven to 250°. Adjust rack to lower third of oven.
2. Combine ¾ cup granulated sugar with walnuts, mixing thoroughly. Butter and flour a large flat baking pan. Trace 2 (9″) circles on the pan.
3. Put egg whites into a clean, grease-free mixing bowl with a small pinch of salt. Begin whipping slowly. When whites are foamy, add cream of tartar. Increase whipping speed. When whites begin hold a soft shape, slowly add ¼ cup sugar. Continue to whip until whites are very stiff, but not dry. Quickly, but gently, fold sugar/nut mixture into egg whites, being careful that whites do not collapse.
4. Fill a large pastry bag fitted with a large #5 tip with meringue mixture. Starting from the center of each traced circle, use a spiral motion to pipe mixture and fill each circle. There should be spaces between spirals when the circle is completed.
5. When both circles are filled, place baking tray in oven at once. Meringues are cooked when discs move when lightly nudged, about 1½ hours. Turn baking tray once half-way through the cooking time. If the meringues darken too quickly, turn the oven to 225°. Cool the meringues on the baking tray as meringues may still be somewhat soft even when they are done.
6. While the meringues are cooking, cream butter and powdered sugar until very light and fluffy. Scrape down sides of bowl from time to time to insure total blending. Combine yolks with heavy cream and add to butter/sugar mixture and continue to beat. Dissolve instant coffee in the Kahlua and add. Scrape bowl again to insure uniform blending.

7. When assembling, handle meringues very carefully as they are extremely fragile. Use the most perfect meringue for the top. Pile buttercream filling onto the bottom circle and smooth evenly until you have a flat surface. Buttercream should extend over the side of the meringue circle. Gently place top meringue circle on the buttercream and press lightly to secure. Using a spatula, smooth excess buttercream on side of cake to fill in any gaps.

8. To garnish, press chopped walnuts onto side of cake. Dust top of cake with powdered sugar until it is totally covered.

*This very unusual and completely delicious recipe was created by my pastry chef, Peter Leary.*

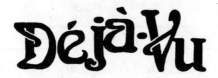

# Déjà-Vu

*Dinner for Six*

Salmon Tartare

Potage Roy-An de Groot

Passion Fruit Sorbet

Entrecôte Déjà-Vu

Salade du Chef

Apple Tart with Frozen Chocolate Mousse and Chocolate Truffles

Wines:

With the Salmon—Dom Pérignon Rosé Champagne, 1969
With the Entrecôte—Château Pétrus, Pomerol, 1959
With the Salade—Sorentberger Edelbeerenauslese, 1969
With the Tart—Cognac, Mme. Gaston Briand

Salomon Montezinos, Owner and Chef

**D**éjà-Vu, aptly named by its creator and chef, Salomon Montezinos, reflects his desire to present his clients with "the sensuality of an absolute experience in taste." He says, "I have tried to realize a vision—a restaurant where the sumptuousness and luxury of another age may join with the relaxed atmosphere of today; an aesthetic experience for the eyes as well as the palate. For me, the difference between a restaurant and a great restaurant is love and tender care. I have lavished both on Déjà-Vu."

The decor is one of unerring elegance, from the baroque beauty of his hand-painted ceilings and walls, to his gleaming silver service, to the warm pink satin chairs to match his specially woven pink linen tablecloths. "I see something beautiful and my mind starts working," says Sal.

Mr. Montezinos trained under the stern Swiss masters in Lucerne, Lausanne, Berne, and St. Moritz. Later, he catered to the diplomatic community and worked for the Holland-America line to broaden his encyclopedic knowledge of local cuisine. Wine has become a passion with the Dutch-born chef and he describes his cellar as "equal even to the demands of my cuisine, with five hundred of the finest select wines from France, Germany, and California. I am," he adds, "the proud owner of the oldest wine cellar in any Philadelphia restaurant, 160 years old."

His cuisine is his own. "I have begun with the techniques of classical French cuisine and adapted them to fit the needs of today. I demand absolute purity of ingredients—I even raise my own ducks to insure their organic purity. I prepare each dish that I serve to order, and I believe in the adventure of delicate and unusual combinations. My goal is perfection and I am constantly striving to blend the dignity of the past with the panache of today to create the ultimate dining experience."

Déjà-Vu offers its clients the fruits of Mr. Montezinos's quest for perfection. Each guest is, for the evening, a cherished visitor, invited to share with him the sensuous luxury of his unique vision.

1609 Pine Street

## SALMON TARTARE

*The salmon in this famous hors d'oeuvre is raw. This regal dish is particularly delicious on a warm summer day when salmon is in season.*

| | | | |
|---|---|---|---|
| 18 | ounces fresh raw salmon | 2 | teaspoons organic ketchup |
| 4 | teaspoons cold-pressed safflower oil | 2 | teaspoons capers, finely minced |
| 2 | teaspoons white wine shallot vinegar | 6 to 12 | anchovies, scraped |
| 1 | teaspoon finely minced fresh chives | 1 | teaspoon finely minced fresh dill |
| 1 | egg yolk | 1 | teaspoon white pepper |
| 1 | teaspoon Dusseldorfer mustard | 1 | teaspoon sea salt |
| 1 to 2 | cloves garlic, finely minced Dash of Hungarian paprika | 3 | ounces cognac |
| | | 1 | loaf homemade whole wheat bread |
| 12 | black peppercorns, crushed (Madagascar preferred) | 1 | lemon, cut into wedges |

1. Slice the salmon into thin slices, removing all skin and bone. Spread out the slices on a flat serving platter.
2. Combine safflower oil, vinegar, and minced chives. Thoroughly sprinkle each slice of salmon. Cover with foil and place a weight on top so the salmon is covered with marinade. Refrigerate for 48 hours. Every 12 hours, carefully lift each slice and turn over so that each slice is completely moistened.
3. After 48 hours, remove from refrigerator. Pour off surplus marinade. Take two towels and lay salmon slices between them. Press gently to absorb the oil. Remove slices from towels and dice.
4. Mix egg yolk, mustard, garlic, paprika, peppercorns, ketchup, capers, anchovies, dill, white pepper, and sea salt in a bowl. Add cognac and salmon, mixing well.
5. Toast thin slices of whole wheat bread and spread with Salmon Tartare. Serve with lemon wedges.

### POTAGE ROY-AN de GROOT

*This soup was invented on the spot during one of "the Baron's" visits to Déjà-Vu.*

4 tablespoons sweet butter
10 pounds organic tomatoes, chopped
  Coarse crystal salt
  Freshly ground black pepper
2 to 3 fresh bay leaves
1 small bunch fresh thyme, minced
1 cucumber, peeled, seeded, finely diced

4 teaspoons coarsely chopped fresh basil
2 teaspoons coarsely chopped fresh chives
2 egg yolks, slightly beaten
½ cup heavy cream
  Carpano Punt e Mes, or red vermouth

1. Preheat oven to 350°.
2. Using a tightly lidded casserole, preferably thick-tinned copper appropriate for use on top of the stove and in the oven, melt butter over medium heat. When melted, add tomatoes and salt. Stir constantly until tomatoes begin to soften, about 10 minutes. Add pepper, bay leaves, and thyme. Stir to mix, and remove from the stove.
3. Set casserole, covered, in center of preheated oven. Allow to stew gently for 1½ hours.
4. Remove casserole from oven. Purée soup in a blender. Pass soup through a coarse sieve, pressing out as much pulp as possible. Return to stove top and add cucumber, basil, chives, egg yolks, and heavy cream. Heat just enough to warm and blend. Taste for seasoning. Pour into individual bowls and add a dash of Punt e Mes to each bowl.

## PASSION FRUIT SORBET

*This superb sorbet is lovely to look at and has an irresistible taste and texture.*

| | |
|---|---|
| 15 ripe fresh passion fruit | 1 lemon, peeled and diced |
| ¾ cup raw turbinado sugar | ½ lime, peeled and diced |
| ½ bottle white wine (preferably German Auslese) | 3 fresh mint leaves |
| | ¼ bottle champagne |

1. Peel the thin outer skin from the passion fruits. Remove seeds and dice. Put in a tinned copper pot. Add sugar, wine, lemon, and lime and bring to a boil, stirring occasionally. Reduce to a simmer and cook for 30 minutes, or as long as it takes to get a good "passion fruity" flavor. Remove from heat and strain through a coarse sieve. Cool.

2. Pour mixture into an ice cream maker and run for 45 minutes to 1 hour or until the desired consistency. If you do not have an ice cream maker, pour mixture into a large container and freeze, stirring occasionally, until mixture is the desired consistency.

3. When ready to serve, fill champagne glasses half full with sorbet. Top each serving with a fresh mint leaf and fill each glass three-fourths of the way to the top with champagne.

*When I serve this elegantly colored sorbet to my guests, I use my best tulip-shaped wine glasses. The champagne I prefer to use is Taittinger Blanc de Blanc, 1971.*

## ENTRECÔTE DÉJÀ-VU

6 (10-ounce) sirloin steaks, 1½" thick
MARINADE (see next page)
½ pound snow peas
3 tablespoons butter
Coarse crystal salt
Nutmeg
Freshly ground white pepper
Freshly ground black pepper
3 tomatoes, cut in half horizontally
½ cup Herbs de Provence
1 cup cold-pressed safflower oil
1 small bunch parsley

1. Cut every scrap of fat away from steaks. Set a heavy frying pan over high heat and add 3 tablespoons Marinade. When butter starts smoking, add the steaks. Turn them over continuously until well browned and crusty on the outside and juicy and rare on the inside. Remove from pan and keep warm on a covered platter in a low oven.
2. Steam or poach the snow peas for 3 to 5 minutes or just until crisp-tender. Strain. Glaze in 2 tablespoons of hot butter and season with salt and nutmeg. Cover and put in a low oven to maintain heat.
3. Salt and pepper the half tomatoes and place on a flat pan. Sprinkle with Herbs de Provence, moisten with remaining butter, and broil for 10 minutes or until lightly browned. Keep warm.
4. Heat the oil in a heavy frying pan to 375°. Dip parsley leaves in and out quickly. Drain on absorbent paper, sprinkle with salt, and keep warm.
5. Take steaks out of oven. Scoop Marinade generously on each steak and broil for about 5 minutes, with rack set so that top surface of Marinade will be 5" from the heat.
6. Serve immediately on very hot plates. Place a steak in the center of each plate and arrange parsley, tomatoes, and snow peas around it.

# DÉJÀ-VU

## MARINADE

1 bunch parsley, chopped
3 scallions, chopped
1 stalk broccoli, trimmed
1 green pepper, cored and diced
1 teaspoon chopped fresh tarragon
½ yellow onion, peeled and chopped
1 bay leaf, crumbled
1 teaspoon chopped thyme
1 small carrot, scraped and chopped
10 cloves garlic, peeled and minced
½ pound spinach leaves, chopped
1 teaspoon chopped chervil
1 bunch watercress, leaves only, chopped
½ teaspoon sweet Hungarian paprika

¼ teaspoon marjoram
1 teaspoon chopped basil
2 teaspoons tomato paste
1 tablespoon capers
¼ cup chopped cornichons
Dash of Tabasco sauce
Pinch of curry powder
12 Portuguese anchovies, drained
2 tablespoons white wine tarragon vinegar
2 tablespoons white wine coriander vinegar
½ tablespoon light soy sauce
2 ounces sweet Marsala
2 tablespoons cognac
1 pound butter
Salt and pepper

1. Two days in advance, combine all herbs and vegetables in a bowl with the tomato paste, capers, cornichons, Tabasco, curry powder, and anchovies. Sprinkle with vinegar, soy sauce, Marsala, and cognac. Mix well, cover, and refrigerate for 24 hours.
2. One day before serving, remove from refrigerator and place in a food processor. Blend until puréed, about 40 seconds. Make sure mixture does not become too mushy. Place back in bowl, cover, and refrigerate overnight.
3. At least 3 hours before serving, beat butter in a mixer until soft and shiny. Add marinade and mix for 15 minutes. Add salt and pepper to taste. Put back into a bowl, cover, and refrigerate for 3 hours or more.

*It is essential to use fresh vegetables and herbs to bring out the delicate flavors of this noble dish.*

## SALADE DU CHEF

3 small heads Bibb lettuce
2 tomatoes, skinned, seeded, and coarsely diced
1 teaspoon fresh bean sprouts, chopped
3 scallions, coarsely chopped
1 medium-size yellow onion, peeled and finely chopped
1 red bell pepper, cored and diced

2 ripe avocados, peeled and sliced into small wedges
*SALAD DRESSING*
1 can hearts of palm, diced (Brazilian preferred)
Salt and pepper

1. Forty-five minutes before serving, wash Bibb lettuce, put in a salad bowl, lightly cover, and refrigerate to crisp and freshen.
2. When ready to serve, add tomatoes, sprouts, scallions, onions, peppers, and avocados to lettuce.
3. Beat dressing slightly and spoon it over the salad. Sprinkle in hearts of palm and toss gently for 1 minute. Grind salt and pepper over the salad. Serve.

### *SALAD DRESSING*

1 egg
1 teaspoon tarragon vinegar
½ teaspoon white wine vinegar
1 teaspoon raw honey
1 teaspoon light soy sauce
2 teaspoons Dijon mustard
Coarse crystal salt

Freshly ground black pepper
4 teaspoons cold-pressed safflower oil
1 tablespoon green, virgin olive oil Provençal

Into a mixing bowl, put the egg, vinegars, honey, soy sauce, mustard, and salt and pepper to taste. Stir to dissolve salt. Add safflower oil and olive oil. Adjust seasonings if necessary. Serve immediately.

*This is an example of the kind of food I prepare. Everything is done to order and served immediately.*

## APPLE TART WITH FROZEN CHOCOLATE MOUSSE AND CHOCLATE TRUFFLES

*The tarts and the mousse should be prepared a day in advance.*

| | |
|---|---|
| 2 tart apples (Granny Smith or Greening) | 1 teaspoon minced crystallized ginger |
| 2½ tablespoons dark Jamaican rum | 1 tablespoon coarsely chopped walnuts |
| 1½ cups sifted unbleached all-purpose flour | FROZEN CHOCOLATE MOUSSE (see next page) |
| ¼ pound unsalted butter | 1 cup whipping cream, whipped and sweetened |
| 1½ cups raw granulated sugar | |
| ½ teaspoon cinnamon | CHOCOLATE TRUFFLES |
| 1 teaspoon seedless raisins | (see second page following) |

1. Thinly slice apples into a bowl. Dribble rum over them. Gently mix with a spoon and marinate, covered, for 30 minutes. Refrigerate.
2. Knead flour, butter, and ½ cup sugar in a mixing bowl for 15 minutes. Work together into a ball, cover with buttered paper and refrigerate for 20 minutes. Meanwhile, lightly butter and flour individual tart pans and preheat oven to 350°.
3. Divide dough equally among each tart mold and spread gently across the bottom and sides with your fingertips. Put a thin layer of apples in each mold and sprinkle with cinnamon, 1 cup sugar, the raisins, ginger, and walnuts. Bake tarts in preheated oven for 20 minutes or until edges are lightly browned. Remove from oven and cool for 30 minutes. Remove tarts from molds and store in a covered container in the refrigerator overnight.
4. When ready to serve, unmold the Mousse and place in tart shells. Decorate the top and sides of each tart by piping on sweetened whipped cream and pressing two truffles onto the sides of the tarts.

### FROZEN CHOCOLATE MOUSSE

2 eggs, beaten
3 egg yolks, beaten
¼ cup sugar
2 tablespoons dark
Jamaican rum
1½ tablespoons finely chopped
Swiss Lindt's Milk
Chocolate with Honey

1½ tablespoons dark semisweet
Dutch Dröste chocolate
1½ cups whipped cream

1. Heat together in a large bowl over a double-boiler the eggs, egg yolks, sugar, and 1 tablespoon rum, stirring gently over medium heat until warm. Transfer to an electric mixer and beat at medium speed until cool and fluffy.
2. Meanwhile, melt both chocolates with remaining rum until mixture is runny. Mix into the egg mixture. Beat for 10 to 15 minutes or until cold.
3. Add whipped cream to the chocolate mixture, folding until well blended. Transfer mousse to tart molds. Cover and freeze overnight.

### CHOCOLATE TRUFFLES

8 ounces white chocolate,
  chopped
1 teaspoon sugar
1 teaspoon rum
½ cup butter, cut into small
  pieces, at room temperature

1 egg yolk
½ cup unsweetened cocoa
  powder

1. Melt white chocolate, sugar, and rum, stirring constantly, until mixture is a smooth consistency. Add butter and stir until cold. Add egg yolk and mix well.
2. Cover and refrigerate until cold. Form into small balls and roll in cocoa powder. Freeze in a container. Remove from freezer one hour before serving.

**deux Cheminées**

*Dinner for Six*

*Velouté Cresson*

*Mousse de Coquilles St. Jacques, Sauce Vin Blanc*

*Foie de Veau Polonaise*

*Mousse de Carottes*

*Gratin Dauphinoise*

*Boule de Neige*

*Wines:*

*With the Mousse—Puligny-Montrachet, Les Combettes, 1978*

*With the Veal—Château Haut-Bailly, Graves, 1976*

*Fritz Blank, Proprietor and Chef*
*Joseph O'Connor, Sous-Chef*
*Roger Johnson, Chef Pâtissier*
*Michelene Grébert, Hôtesse*
*James Petrie, Manager*

# *DEUX CHEMINÉES*

Deux Cheminées is unique in several ways. Although it has only been open for two years, it has already acquired a four-star rating in the *Mobil Guide*. Its owner and chef, Fritz Blank, is a microbiologist, formerly director of the microbiology department at Crozer Chester Medical Center and is even now on the faculty of the Hahneman Medical Center. Its atmosphere is singularly private. Fritz describes it as "an understated but elegant home." He adds, "We'd like our guests to feel as if they were dining at friends'."

Mr. Blank explains his decision to change careers: "I always loved to cook and I entertained constantly. I studied with Julie Danenbaum for a number of years, yet considered cooking only an avocation until I was literally catapulted into Deux Cheminées by an associate who was looking for an investment. In making the transition from private cook to restaurateur, I was lucky to have the assistance of my sous-chef, Joseph O'Connor, who came from the Garden. He was my bridge in the leap from a single Bunsen burner to a twelve-top stove."

The food at Deux Cheminées is traditional regional French. Fritz says, "I am constantly on the lookout for new recipes, as well as adapting and changing my old ones. I hope that I will never stop learning—and creating."

Deux Cheminées is housed in an historically certified townhouse built in the early nineteenth century, which later became the site of the first French restaurant in Philadelphia, La Coin d'Or. The spirit of the original home has been carefully restored, from the roaring fire in the vestibule to the continued use of the original dumbwaiter, more than one hundred fifty years old. New touches have been added, such as the magnificent stained-glass ceiling on the second floor, salvaged from the old Taft Hotel in New York.

The atmosphere at Deux Cheminées is warm and gracious, aided by the charming hostess, Micheline Grébert, who greets everyone personally as they arrive. Fritz Blanc is a superb host—offering magnificent cuisine in an intimate and welcoming setting.

251 Camac Street

## VELOUTÉ CRESSON (Froide ou Chaude)

2 *bunches watercress*
1½ *cups chopped onion*
2 *tablespoons butter*
   *Salt and pepper*

*SAUCE VELOUTÉ*
2 *egg yolks*
   *Watercress or carrot curls*

1. Prepare watercress by trimming off stems.
2. Sauté onions and butter in stock pot until onions are transparent. Add watercress and cook until it wilts. Add 1½ cups of water, salt, and pepper. Bring to a boil. Remove from heat.
3. Purée in batches in food procesor, leaving texture slightly rough.
4. Combine with Sauce Velouté and season again with salt and pepper. Beat in egg yolks. Insert bowl into a larger container filled with ice so that soup will chill rapidly. Serve garnished with watercress or carrot curls.

*This soup may be prepared in advance and stored in the refrigerator after initial chilling, to be served hot or cold. If you plan to serve it hot, heat gently. Once the egg yolks are added, the soup will curdle if it is allowed to boil.*

### SAUCE VELOUTÉ

2 *tablespoons flour*
2 *tablespoons butter*
4 *cups chicken stock*

2 *cups milk*
1 *cup heavy cream*

1. Create a roux by cooking flour and butter in a heavy saucepan over medium heat for 2 to 3 minutes, stirring constantly with a wooden spoon. The roux is done when a haze forms on the bottom of the pan after it is scraped by the spoon.
2. Slowly add chicken stock, stirring with a whisk over medium heat, watching carefully so that the bottom does not scorch. Add milk and cream and bring to boil. Remove from heat.

### MOUSSE DE COQUILLES ST. JACQUES

*This recipe will make 1½ quarts of terrine, which may be kept for one week.*

| | |
|---|---|
| 2 pounds sea scallops | Salt and pepper |
| 3 egg whites | 2 to 2¾ cups heavy cream |
| 1 tablespoon dry vermouth, gin, or cognac | 1 tablespoon butter |
| | SAUCE VIN BLANC |
| 1 whole egg | 1 lemon, sliced |
| 2 tablespoons chopped tarragon | ½ bunch watercress, or ½ bunch parsley |

1. Purée raw scallops in food processor until smooth. Add egg whites, one at a time. Add vermouth, whole egg, and tarragon, continuing to process. Taste, adding salt and pepper as needed.
2. Transfer to a mixer, using flat paddle at medium speed. Add heavy cream slowly, until the consistency is such that the mixture will plop off a spoon held 6" above bowl.
3. Using a 1½-quart terrine (heavy cast iron coated with enamel), cut a piece of waxed paper to fit the top. Butter terrine well and fill with mousse. Put well-buttered waxed paper, buttered side down, on top of mousse to keep it from scorching. Cover with lid an insert terrine into a bain-marie (a larger pot filled with water). The water level should be ⅔ of the way to the top of the terrine. Bake at 350° for 35 to 45 minutes. The mousse should feel springy to the touch when cooking is completed.
4. Remove from oven. Allow to set for 5 to 10 minutes.
5. Nap the bottom of a serving plate by pouring Sauce Vin Blanc onto the bottom. Slice mousse and put on plate, garnishing with lemon slices, watercress, or parsley.

*This very versatile recipe may also be refrigerated. After it has been chilled, unmold, slice ½" to 1" thick, put in pan, cover with tin foil, and reheat at 350° for 8 to 10 minutes. Always serve warm. If desired, green peppercorns may be substituted for tarragon, to give the terrine a certain élan. Or, half the mousse may be poured into the terrine and a layer of scallops, shrimp, or lobster—or of julienned carrots and celery—may be added and then covered with the rest of the mousse.*

### SAUCE VIN BLANC

6 to 9  mussels
    1  cup white wine
    2  cups water
    1  cup FISH STOCK (see
      next page)
  1⅓  cups vermouth

1  tablespoon chopped shallots
6  mushrooms, sliced
2  cups heavy cream
4  tablespoons softened butter
   A few drops of lemon juice

1. To create mussel broth, clean and scrub mussels. Steam in white wine and water. Cook until mussels open. Reserve liquid and remove mussels from shells.
2. To 2 cups of mussel broth, add Fish Stock, vermouth, shallots, mushrooms, and mussels. Reduce gently for approximately 1 hour or until mixture has reduced to about one-fourth of its original amount. Remove from heat and add heavy cream. Return to heat over low flame and cook for about 10 minutes or until sauce coats the back of a spoon.
3. Strain in a strainer lined with cheesecloth. Finish by adding butter and lemon juice.

*Before adding heavy cream, you have created a flavor essence. After adding heavy cream, sauce may be refrigerated for as long as a week, but after butter is added, it must be served. After adding cream, be careful to use gentle heat or the sauce will break. If this happens, the sauce cannot be "repaired" and must then be started all over again.*

## FISH STOCK

| | |
|---|---|
| 2 *cups white wine* | ½ *carrot, chopped* |
| 5 *washed fish bones,* | ½ *stalk celery, chopped* |
| *preferably swordfish,* | ½ *teaspoon fennel seeds* |
| *including heads, tails,* | ½ *lemon* |
| *skins and trimmings* | ½ *bay leaf* |
| ½ *onion, chopped* | ½ *teaspoon black peppercorns* |

Simmer all ingredients together with enough water to cover for 2 hours, skimming often. Strain.

*Your local fishmonger will be able to give you the fish bones.*

## FOIE DE VEAU POLONAISE

*I call this recipe Polonaise because it was given to me by a Polish lady. In its original form, it used pork liver and cider vinegar.*

| | |
|---|---|
| 3 *pounds calves liver* | 3 *ounces demi-glace* |
| 5 *tablespoons butter* | *(see index)* |
| 1 *cup flour* | 1 *tablespoon parsley* |
| 3 *tablespoons chopped* | *Saslt and pepper* |
| *shallots* | 6 *fresh raspberries* |
| 3 *ounces raspberry vinegar* | |

1. Slice liver into medallions ½" thick and 3" in diameter.
2. Melt 3 tablespoons butter in sauté pan. Dip liver in flour and sauté until medium rare, about 3 minutes per side. Remove to heated plate.
3. Discard butter in pan. Add shallots, vinegar, demi-glace, parsley, salt and pepper. De-glaze pan by scraping with a wooden spoon and stirring. Reduce mixture to half over medium-high heat for about 3 minutes.
4. Add remaining butter and mix in. Pour sauce over liver. Garnish with a fresh raspberry on each medallion.

*If you overcook liver, it will be too tough. Well-done liver is blasphemy—like shoe leather.*

# DEUX CHEMINÉES

## MOUSSE DE CAROTTES

*This very distinctive dish may be made in advance and reheated over a low heat. You must be careful not to scorch. Beurre noisette may also be used with peas, broccoli, or cauliflower to create an unusual nutty taste.*

| | |
|---|---|
| 2 pounds carrots | 6 tablespoons butter |
| 1 orange, sliced in half | ¼ cup Grand Marnier |
| ⅓ cup sugar | Chopped parsley |

1. Wash, trim, and slice carrots. Place in a saucepan with orange, sugar, and enough water to barely cover carrots. Boil until tender. Remove orange and drain carrots.
2. Burn butter in a sauté pan, creating a beurre noisette.
3. Put beurre noisette and carrots in a food processor and purée. Add Grand Marnier and mix well. Serve garnished with chopped parsley.

### GRATIN DAUPHINOIS

*Contrary to popular belief,* gratin *means a browned crumb mixture. It need not mean that cheese is added, although I have done so in this case.*

| | |
|---|---|
| 8 medium-large Maine potatoes | Salt and pepper |
| 2 tablespoons butter | 1½ cups heavy cream |
| 4 leeks, white part only, chopped | ¼ to ½ cup shredded Jarlsberg cheese |
| 1 bunch fresh parsley, chopped | |

1. Peel and thinly slice potatoes. Keep in cold water until ready for use.
2. Preheat oven to 325°.
3. Use 1 tablespoon butter to butter a 1½" deep copper gratin pan. Arrange a layer of potatoes, a layer of leeks, and another layer of potatoes, sprinkling each layer with parsley and salt and pepper. Pour in heavy cream until it covers three-fourths of the pan depth. Sprinkle the top with cheese, being careful not to smother with too much cheese. Dot with remaining butter.
4. Insert gratin pan into a bain-marie. Bake in preheated oven for 45 minutes to 1 hour. Serve.

*Maine potatoes are the best to use because their texture allows them to fully absorb the cream.*

## BOULE DE NEIGE

*This superb dessert is very rich yet it remains light because it contains no flour. It is named boule de neige because it looks like half of a giant snowball when it is served. The recipe is from the* Maida Heater Chocolate Cook Book *and she gives credit to Abby Mandell, the Cuisinart cooking wizard.*

½ cup water
2 teaspoons instant coffee powder
½ pound butter
½ pound semisweet chocolate (Peter's Coating Chocolate is recommended)

1 cup sugar
4 whole eggs
1 tablespoon dark rum
RUM-FLAVORED WHIPPED CREAM

1. Preheat oven to 350°.
2. Combine water and coffee in a saucepan and add the butter, chocolate, and sugar. Heat over a low heat, stirring constantly, until chocolate and butter have melted.
3. Put mixture in food processor. Using the steel blade, add eggs one at a time. Add rum.
4. Line a 2-quart rounded-bottom ovenproof bowl with tin foil. Butter the sides and the bottom of the tin foil. Add chocolate mixture and bake in preheated oven for 35 minutes. The cake will rise and the top will have a cracked appearance. Remove cake from oven. As it cools, the middle will fall. Press down with hands each time that happens so that top of the cake is lightly compressed and remains flat.
5. Refrigerate overnight. The cake may be left in the refrigerator for 1 week, or frozen.
6. To serve, unmold by putting a plate on top and inverting. Cover with Rum Flavored Whipped Cream, applied with a star-tip pastry bag.

### *RUM-FLAVORED WHIPPED CREAM*

1 pint whipping cream
1 tablespoon confectioners' sugar

½ tablespoon rum

Whip ingredients together until stiff.

*Dinner for Six*

*Garden Salad*

*Bouillabaisse Dockside*

*Crème Caramel*

*Wines:*

*With the Salad—Sherry, Tío Pepe, Gonzalez Byass*

*With the Bouillabaise—a California Cabernet Sauvignon*

*With the Custard—Sauternes, Barton et Guestier, France, 1976*

*Barry Nachimson and David Mink, Owners and Chefs*

# DOCKSIDE FISH CO.

The Dockside Fish Company is an unpretentious neighborhood restaurant that "attracts diners from all over the Delaware Valley." As Barry Nachimson, the co-owner and a former practicing attorney, says, "What we offer is very simple. We are neither quaint nor trendy—we merely present the best and freshest fish cooked in the most appetizing way, at a reasonable price. Our goal is to become the number one fish restaurant in Philadelphia."

His unusual partnership with David Mink was cemented in a hot tub over a bottle of wine. Barry describes it as follows, "David and his family have been in the restaurant business as long as David can remember. He provides the expertise and I, the physical presence and management. I am always here to greet our customers, many of whom have become friends. I'm a very straightforward man and I try to run our restaurant in the same way."

David believes that one of their strengths is that they are both always on the lookout for new recipes and suppliers. "It was my family that first brought Belon oysters to Philadelphia. Now we are serving sea urchins at the Dockside Fish Company. Even when I go on vacation, I make sure that I am near a place where I can fish and talk to other fishermen. If I am particularly lucky and catch enough, we'll even serve *my* fish at the restaurant."

One of the specialties at the Dockside Fish Company is char-grilled fish, cooked on an open-grated grill. "If the fish is fresh—and we buy ours daily and in small quantities—the simplest means of preparation is often the most delicious," says Barry.

The decor is simple, clean, and airy. In an understated and subtle way, the warm beige walls with a touch of lavender at the top molding create the ambiance of a flowing ocean. "One of the nicer things about our dining room," says Barry, "is that one whole wall is windowed. You can sit anywhere and look outside."

The Dockside Fish Company is an excellent place to enjoy one of Philadelphia's specialties—fresh fish—served in a relaxed yet delectable manner.

815 Locust Street

# DOCKSIDE FISH CO.

### GARDEN SALAD

1 large head romaine, torn
  into bite-size pieces
1 large carrot, thinly sliced
1 cucumber with skin on,
  thinly sliced
½ bunch radishes, cleaned
  and thinly sliced

18 cherry tomatoes, halved
  VINAIGRETTE
1 red onion, thinly sliced
  Black pitted olives

Toss romaine, carrot, cucumber, radishes and tomatoes with Vinaigrette. Garnish with onion and olives.

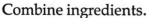

### *VINAIGRETTE*

1½ cups olive oil
½ cup red wine vinegar
½ teaspoon garlic powder
½ teaspoon dry mustard

¼ teaspoon black pepper
½ teaspoon sugar
¼ teaspoon salt

Combine ingredients.

# DOCKSIDE FISH CO.

## BOUILLABAISSE DOCKSIDE

*Our recipe is an adaptation of the recipe presented in the book entitled* Creole Gumbo and All That Jazz *written by our friend, Howard Mitcham. As Mitch says, 'The three hallmarks of a good bouillabaisse are: 1) It should be garlicky as hell. 2) It should be a golden yellow color and have a slight flavor of iodine from the saffron. 3) The fish should not be over-cooked and the dish should have a fresh tang of the salt sea in it.'*

| | |
|---|---|
| ¾ cup olive oil | 2 dozen littleneck clams in their shells |
| 1½ large onions, chopped | |
| 8 cloves garlic, minced | 2 dozen mussels in their shells |
| 3 scallions, chopped | |
| 2¼ large tomatoes, peeled and chopped (¾ of a 16-ounce can may be substituted) | 1 pint shucked oysters |
| | 3 chicken lobsters (less than 1 pound each) |
| 2¼ teaspoons chopped parsley | FISH STOCK |
| ⅜ teaspoon powdered saffron | Salt and freshly ground black pepper |
| 1 pound mackerel fillet | |
| 1 pound rockfish fillet | |

1. Heat the olive oil in a 3-quart pot. Cook the onions, garlic, scallions, tomatoes, and parsley until soft and transparent, for approximately 5 minutes. Stir in the saffron. Add the fish fillets, the shellfish, well scrubbed, and the lobsters, split in half, to the pot. Add enough Fish Stock to cover the ingredients by two inches. If there is not enough Fish Stock, add water. Bring the mixture to a boil and cook for a few minutes. You will know it is done when the littleneck clams and mussels open and the lobster shells have turned red. Taste the broth and add salt and pepper if necessary.

2. Bring to the table in a large covered tureen. Ladle half a lobster in each soup plate with lots of "goodies" and the broth.

*This dish is hearty and satisfying for those long winter nights. It provides you with a complete balanced meal. All you need is a coarse crusty bread, a good Cabernet Sauvignon, and a crackling fire close by.*

# DOCKSIDE FISH CO.

### FISH STOCK

3 pounds fish heads and bones

3 quarts water

1½ large onions, coarsely chopped

2¼ tomatoes, coarsely chopped (¾ of a 16-ounce can may be substituted)

1½ ribs celery with leaves, coarsley chopped

¾ cup parsley sprigs

1½ bay leaves

½ lemon, sliced

⅜ teaspoon thyme

⅜ teaspoon basil

⅜ teaspoon freshly ground black pepper

¼ teaspoon cayenne

1 tablespoon salt

Place all ingredients in a pot and boil vigorously for 30 minutes. Strain through a colander strainer or a triple cheesecloth, extracting as much as possible. Reserve the stock and discard the solid waste.

## CRÈME CARAMEL

¾ cup sugar

3 eggs

Pinch of salt

1 tablespoon vanilla extract

2 cups hot milk

1. Melt ½ cup sugar in a saucepan until sugar caramelizes (melts and turns brown). Pour the syrup into 6 ramekins. Let sit for 5 minutes.
2. Slightly beat the eggs, add salt and remaining sugar, and stir until the sugar has dissolved. Add vanilla. Gradually pour milk into the mixture, stirring constantly. Pour into the 6 ramekins, diving the mixture equally. Place the ramekins in a pan of hot water and bake in a moderate oven at 325° for 30 to 45 minutes, or until the crème caramels are firm in the center. Test with a knife; when the knife comes out clean, the dessert is done.
3. Allow to cool and then refrigerate. Before serving, place each crème caramel in a shallow dish filled with hot water, wait for one minute to allow the caramel to loosen, and turn upside down on a dessert dish.

*This traditional New Orleans dessert, called cup custard, is a perfect finale to the bouillabaisse—light, sweet, and not fattening.*

*Dinner for Six*

*Cream of Mushroom Soup*

*Seafood Strudel*

*Watercress and Endive Salad*

*Roast Duck in Curry Sauce*

*Strawberry Kiwi Tart*

*Wines:*

*With the Strudel—Preston Vineyards Sauvignon Blanc, 1980*
*With the Duck—Lytton Springs Zinfandel, 1979*
*With the Tart—Schramsberg Blanc de Noirs champagne, 1977*

*Weaver Lilly, Proprietor*
*William Weaver, Chef*

Friday Saturday Sunday prides itself on being a neighborhood restaurant. As owner Weaver Lilley says, "Most of our clients walk here and come frequently. As a result, they have become our friends. In fact, many of them enter through the kitchen and stop to talk to the chef on their way in."

The cuisine is what Chef William Weaver calls "bourgeoisie food"— "a modified peasant style that is neither heavy nor light." He values the use of a blackboard for the menu because it gives him the creative opportunity to change frequently. He says, "Our menu totally reflects what is available at the market, so we must change it often. After all, no one wants to eat the same thing all the time. Our only problem is that our regular customers refuse to let us omit their favorites."

Started nine years ago as a lark by photographer Lilley, Friday Saturday Sunday quickly hit its stride on the crest of the new wave of Philadelphia restaurants, despite the fact that it didn't have a liquor license for three years. "It was an excellent discipline for us," says Lilley. "We had to be able to function as a restaurant based completely on the quality of our food. Now that we are a 'grown-up restaurant,' I have become very involved in wine selection and take great pride in the quality of our cellar."

From the deep maroon, fully restored pick-up truck, reminiscent of the Bonnie and Clyde era and used for daily visits to the market, to the salt-water fish tank in the upstairs bar, to the canopied ceilings, Friday Saturday Sunday projects an easy, relaxed charm. Such an event as the recent Beaujolais Nouveau Fête celebrating the arrival of the new, short-lived wine exemplify the élan and joi de vivre of this delightful restaurant.

261 South 21st Street

## CREAM OF MUSHROOM SOUP

1 pound mushrooms, finely
  chopped
4 tablespoons butter
4 tablespoons flour

1 quart chicken stock
1 quart heavy cream
¼ cup sherry
  Salt and pepper

1. Sauté mushrooms in butter over medium heat for 2 to 3 minutes or until they have released their moisture. Add flour and incorporate well. Add chicken stock and let reduce over medium heat by one-half, approximately 90 minutes.
2. Add heavy cream, sherry, salt and pepper. Mix well and serve.

*This extra-rich soup can be prepared a day in advance and refrigerated before adding the cream, sherry, salt and pepper. To serve, simply re-heat gently while stirring and adding the remaining ingredients.*

## SEAFOOD STRUDEL

1 onion, finely chopped
1 teaspoon butter
1½ cups mixed seafood, sliced
(scallops that have been
lightly poached, lobster
meat, cooked shrimp,
crabmeat)
4 ounces cream cheese

2 teaspoons dry mustard
2 teaspoons chopped parsley
1 teaspoon lemon juice
Salt and pepper
8 sheets phyllo dough
½ cup melted butter
½ cup fine bread crumbs

1. Sauté onion in 1 teaspoon of butter for 4 to 5 minutes. Do not let it brown. Add seafood and sauté for a few minutes. Add softened cream cheese and season with mustard, parsley, lemon juice, salt and pepper. Reserve.

2. Preheat oven to 375°.

3. Begin working with phyllo sheets, one at a time, keeping the remaining sheets covered with a damp, but not wet towel. Brush each sheet with melted butter and sprinkle with bread crumbs. Repeat with remaining sheets, stacking one on top of the other until you have 4 sheets. Spoon seafood mixture 1" from bottom of the sheets lengthwise down the whole sheet. Leave a 1" margin on each end. Roll the seafood mixture up jelly-roll style. Place the roll on a sheet pan, brush with melted butter and sprinkle with breadcrumbs. Repeat process with the remaining 4 phyllo sheets. You will now have 2 complete rolls, each the thickness of 4 phyllo sheets.

4. Slit the tops of the rolls into 6 serving pieces before baking in preheated oven for 20 minutes. Serve two pieces for each portion.

*This dish, one of my favorites, can also be served as an entrée.*

## WATERCRESS AND ENDIVE SALAD

2 bunches watercress with
  2" of the stems removed
  *VINAIGRETTE*

3 Belgian endives with
  sheaves separated
1 bunch radishes, sliced

1. Toss watercress leaves in Vinaigrette. Toss endives in Vinaigrette.
2. Place endive sheaves on chilled plates in a star pattern. Place watercress on top of endive. Sprinkle with sliced radishes.

### *VINAIGRETTE*

1 cup olive oil
4 tablespoons Dijon mustard
¼ cup red wine vinegar
¼ cup white wine

Pinch of chopped thyme
Pinch of chopped fresh
  tarragon
Pinch of chopped parsley

Whisk the oil into the mustard. Slowly add the red wine vinegar and white wine. Add seasonings.

*The Vinaigrette may be made ahead of time. It simply will not taste the same without fresh tarragon. This salad is particularly colorful with the green watercress, red radishes, and white endives.*

## ROAST DUCK IN CURRY SAUCE

3 (3-pound) ducks, cleaned
Salt and pepper
3 carrots

3 stalks celery
3 onions, quartered
CURRY SAUCE

1. Pre-heat oven to 400°.
2. Prepare the ducks for roasting by seasoning the cleaned inside cavity with salt and pepper. Place one carrot, a celery stalk, and several onion quarters inside the cavity of each duck. Put ducks in roasting pan and roast in preheated oven for 1½ hours. Remove and let cool.
3. Prepare for final roasting and crisping by splitting the ducks in half. Remove breast bone and ribs. Place in a 450° oven for 30 minutes to crisp.
4. Serve covered with Curry Sauce.

### CURRY SAUCE

½ cup sugar
½ cup red wine vinegar
1 quart orange juice
2 cups honey
1 medium-size onion, sliced

1 red bell pepper, sliced
1 green pepper, sliced
2 tablespoons butter
4 tablespoons curry powder

1. Caramelize the sugar and red wine vinegar by bringing to a full boil and allowing sugar to get brown, but not burnt. Add the orange juice and honey.
2. Sauté the sliced onion and peppers in butter over medium heat for 4 to 5 minutes or until soft, stirring occasionally. Add to the above mixture. Add curry powder and reduce at medium heat for 40 minutes, stirring occasionally.

*The sauce may be thickened with cornstarch if the consistency is not right.*

### STRAWBERRY KIWI TART

| | |
|---|---|
| ¾ *pound cream cheese* | ½ *cup heavy cream* |
| 10½ *tablespoons butter* | ½ *cup apricot preserves* |
| 1¼ *cups flour* | 2 *kiwi fruits, thinly sliced* |
| 4 *eggs* | 15 *strawberries, thinly* |
| *Grated zest and juice of* | *sliced lengthwise* |
| *2 lemons* | |

1. Pre-heat oven to 350°.
2. Blend ¼ pound of cream cheese, the butter, and flour together in a food processor until it forms a ball. Roll out on floured board and line a deep-dish quiche pan with the dough. Bake shell in preheated oven until it is two-thirds of the way done, or 5 to 10 minutes. Cool.
3. Process ½ pound cream cheese, eggs, lemon zest and juice, and heavy cream in a blender until smooth. Pour into pie shell and bake in 350° oven until set, approximately 45 minutes. Remove and allow to cool.
4. Meanwhile, melt apricot preserves over low heat. Strain and set aside.
5. Arrange kiwi and strawberries in alternating circles on top of filling. Glaze top with melted and strained apricot preserves. Chill and serve.

*This light and piquant fruit tart is a rare combination of classical techniques and new touches.*

# FRÖG

*Dinner for Four*

*Buckwheat Pasta Salad with Julienned Vegetables*

*Noisettes of Lamb with Raspberry Vinegar Sauce*

*Grilled Chèvre Montrachet with Tomato Chutney*

*Mocha Butter Crunch Pie*

*Wines:*

*With the Salad—Clos du Bois Gewürztraminer*

*With the Lamb and Cheese—Chateau Montelena Zinfandel*

*Steven Poses, Owner*
*Bob Maranville, Chef*

## FRÖG

**F**rög, open for eight-and-a-half years, has been described as "the first of the new kind of boutique restaurant in Philadelphia." Chef Bob Maranville, like most of the rest of the senior staff, finds Frög "an exciting place to work.

"In this crazy business," he says, "Frög is the most adventuresome and challenging place I can think of to be. We're the trend-setters. Never pretentious and always creative, we reflect entirely the genius of our owner, Steven Poses.

"Our menu," Bob says, "is what we like to call Philadelphia Cuisine. Since I am prone to excess, I keep adding new dishes constantly. One thing remains absolute. If fresh food is not available in the market, it will not be served here. We never skimp and we always insist on the top of the line."

Last year, Frög moved to more spacious quarters. Bob describes the move as follows: "Frög has grown up. We are two-thirds bigger than we were when we started. We all participated in the planning, and the day I saw them lay the tiles in my new kitchen, I felt like a kid on Christmas day."

The decor is urbane, subtly sophisticated and understated. From the original works of art on the wall to the orchids in hand-turned pots found at each table, no effort was spared "to make our clients comfortable." Says Bob, "We even have a no smoking area. We don't want anything to interfere with our guests' enjoyment of their meal. After all, if you like people, as I do, working at a restaurant is almost like throwing a continuous party. Thanks to Steven's style of management, all of us here feel as if we are partners in a joint enterprise, which makes the quality of food and service excellent."

Intimate and airy, a quixotic blend of the Oriental and the French in both decor and cuisine, Frög is an ideally relaxed choice for the diner who demands both elegance and charm.

1524 Locust Street

## BUCKWHEAT PASTA SALAD WITH JULIENNE VEGETABLES

1 pound buckwheat pasta
3 tablespoons sesame oil
½ teaspoon salt
½ teaspoon pepper
  DRESSING
¾ cup julienned carrots

¾ cup julienned red peppers
¾ cup julienned zucchini
¾ cup julienned snow peas
1 cup sliced mushrooms
½ head romaine or red cabbage

1. Cook pasta in rapidly boiling water for 3 to 4 minutes. Drain and rinse in cold water. When drained, after 3 or 4 minutes, toss with sesame oil, salt, and pepper.
2. Just before serving, toss the pasta with the Dressing and vegetables. Serve in a small bowl lined with romaine or red cabbage leaves.

### *DRESSING*

½ cup soy sauce
½ cup rice or cider vinegar
½ cup corn oil
¼ cup sesame oil
1 tablespoon minced fresh ginger

1 tablespoon minced fresh garlic
2 tablespoons sugar
2 teaspoons pepper

Combine all ingredients.

*The dressing for this salad may be stored in the refrigerator for up to one month. Seafood or chicken may be substituted for or added to the vegetables. This versatile salad allows for great flexibility on the part of the cook.*

## NOISETTES OF LAMB WITH RASPBERRY VINEGAR SAUCE

| | |
|---|---|
| 1 rack of lamb | 2 tablespoons pink peppercorns |
| 6 ounces clarified butter | |
| 1½ teaspoons salt | 2 tablespoons finely chopped shallots |
| 1¼ teaspoons pepper | |
| ½ cup plus 1 tablespoon flour | ¼ cup brown sauce (2 tablespoons Bovril may be substituted) |
| 1 cup burgundy | |
| 1 cup raspberry vinegar | |
| | ¼ pound sweet butter |
| | ½ bunch watercress sprigs |

1. Have the butcher prepare the lamb by removing the loins from the bone and trimming away all of the fat. The loins should be cut into 16 (1½-ounce) slices.

2. Heat clarified butter in a sauté pan until very hot. Add 1 teaspoon salt and 1 teaspoon pepper to flour and dredge noisettes in the seasoned flour, shaking off the excess. Sauté noisettes for approximately 1½ minutes on each side. If you do not have a pan large enough to sauté all the noisettes simultaneously, simply use half the clarified butter for eight at a time. Remove noisettes after cooking to a heated plate in a 200° oven.

3. Discard all but 1 tablespoon drippings in the pan. Add 1 tablespoon flour to the pan and stir with the drippings, cooking for approximately 3 minutes on low heat. Add burgundy, vinegar, 1 tablespoon peppercorns, ½ teaspoon salt, ¼ teaspoon ground pepper, shallots, and brown sauce. Reduce liquid to ¾ cup, about 15 to 20 minutes, and whisk in sweet butter.

4. Pour sauce over noisettes. Garnish with remaining peppercorns and watercress sprigs.

*This should be served with wild rice or roasted potatoes. Green beans, sautéed in butter with shallots, make an excellent side dish.*

## GRILLED CHÈVRE MONTRACHET WITH TOMATO CHUTNEY

2 cups hickory chips
2 tablespoons finely chopped fresh parsley
½ teaspoon freshly ground cumin seed
1 teaspoon chopped fresh oregano leaves
1 teaspoon chopped fresh chives
1 teaspoon chopped fresh marjoram
1 teaspoon chopped fresh thyme
½ teaspoon freshly ground black pepper
1 log Chèvre Montrachet (with or without ash)
1 cup olive oil
16 pieces melba toast
Tomato Chutney (see next page)
Fresh sprigs of rosemary or sage

1. Light hibachi or charcoal grill 1 hour before cheese is to be grilled. Soak hickory chips in 3 cups cold water for 50 minutes. Add the chips to coals, spreading them evenly over the top 10 minutes before cheese is to be grilled.
2. Combine all the herbs. Roll cheese in herb mixture and wrap cheese in a 12" by 14" piece of cheesecloth, securing the cloth with twine as one would a roast. Soak cheesecloth ball in olive oil.
3. Place cheese on grill and roll over the charcoals using a spatula. Roll frequently and grill for 30 minutes. The cloth will become somewhat charred.
4. Cool cheese to room temperature and remove string and cheese-cloth. Slice into 12 medallions. Serve with fresh melba toast and Tomato Chutney and garnish with sprigs of fresh rosemary, sage, or other herb.

*Fresh herbs, a good quality of olive oil, and the hickory chips add a definite flavor to this unusual dish.*

## TOMATO CHUTNEY

1 cup diced under-ripe
  tomatoes
1 medium-size onion, diced
2 tablespoons kosher salt
2 cups cider vinegar
1 green pepper
1 red pepper
2 apples
2 cloves garlic, minced

1 cup brown sugar
½ teaspoon dried mustard
½ teaspoon salt
½ teaspoon whole cloves
1 stick cinnamon
½ teaspoon powdered ginger
  (or 1 teaspoon minced
  fresh ginger)

1. Combine tomatoes and onion. Sprinkle with kosher salt and let stand in the refrigerator for 12 hours. Remove, rinse in clear water, and drain. Remove tomato seeds and membranes.
2. Heat vinegar to boiling. Add the tomatoes and onion. Seed and dice peppers. Peel, seed, and dice apples. Add to vinegar.
3. Add spices and simmer for 30 minutes, stirring frequently. Cool to room temperature. Remove cinnamon stick and store chutney in refrigerator.

*The tomato chutney will keep for several months in the refrigerator.*

## MOCHA BUTTER CRUNCH PIE

*The choice of bitter or sweet chocolate for the pie crust should reflect the preference of the cook. We find that both are equally popular.*

1 cup flour
¼ teaspoon salt
⅓ cup brown sugar
⅓ cup butter
3 tablespoons chopped
  chocolate, bitter or sweet
¾ cup chopped walnuts

4 to 5 tablespoons water
2 teaspoons vanilla
FILLING
ICING
1½ tablespoons grated
  chocolate

# FRÖG

1. Preheat oven to 350°.
2. Mix flour, salt and brown sugar in a bowl. Cut in butter with a pastry blender. With a fork, stir in chocolate, walnuts, 2 to 3 tablespoons water, and 1 teaspoon vanilla. Mix remaining vanilla and water together and toss in. This mixture will be very crumbly. With floured fingers, press the dough into a 9″ pie pan that is not too deep. It is essential to push the dough up and onto the rim of the pan so that it will not shrink down the sides while baking. Bake in a preheated oven for 15 to 20 minutes. Cool.
3. Pour Filling mixture into pie shell and chill for several hours.
4. Pipe Icing through a pastry bag with a large star tip, creating large rosettes over the entire surface of the pie. Garnish with grated chocolate.

*To "cut" is one of the most basic steps in pastry preparation—"cut"implies cutting into small pieces without actually mixing to homogeneity.*

### FILLING

| | |
|---|---|
| ½ pound unsalted butter | 2 teaspoons vanilla |
| 1 cup brown sugar | 3 ounces bitter chocolate, melted |
| 4 teaspoons powdered instant coffee | 4 eggs |

1. Cream butter until very fluffy and completely smooth. Add brown sugar, instant coffee, and vanilla. Continue to cream so that mixture remains very smooth. Add melted chocolate.
2. Add eggs, one at a time, beating for 3 to 5 minutes after each addition.

### ICING

| | |
|---|---|
| 2 cups whipping cream | ½ cup powdered sugar |
| 7 teaspoons powdered instant coffee | |

Make sure cream is very cold. Combine with instant coffee and sugar, beating until mixture is stiff enough to hold its shape.

THE GARDEN

*Dinner for Four*

*Malpeque, Wellfleet, Cotuit, and Belon Oysters*

*Roast Baby Squab on Croutons with Foie Gras*

*Celery Root Purée*

*Endive, Watercress, and Walnut Salad with Roquefort Dressing*

*White Chocolate Mousse in Almond Baskets with Strawberry Purée*

*Wines:*
*With the Oysters—Robert Mondavi Fumé Blanc Reserve, 1978*

*With the Squab—Chateau Montelena Cabernet Sauvignon, 1975*

*With the Mousse—Schramsberg Blanc de Blancs, 1978*

*Kathleen Mulhern, Owner and Chef*
*Christina Pappajohn, Testing Chef*

# THE GARDEN

**K**athleen Mulhern, the owner of the Garden, says, "It was the garden that sold me on the old Musical Academy building. I could visualize the serendipity of a festive garden in the middle of downtown Philadelphia." Her intuition has been realized. From the canopied part of the garden, where one can sit and listen to the rain pattering overhead, to the open garden, with yellow umbrellas and black tables, climbing roses and lush potted plants, her patrons are treated to a rare opportunity for al fresco dining.

Ms. Mulhern has maintained the intensely personal character of her garden inside the restaurant. Her collections of old, working swan decoys, Currier and Ives trotting prints, and George Brookshaw botanicals highlight the many large and small rooms available for fine dining. Her eye for detail is fine—down to the authentic French garb of her staff—and can be measured by the many awards and testimonies from wine and food societies which line her entrance hall.

Ms. Mulhern describes her cuisine as utilizing "the finest of American ingredients with a touch of Gallic know-how. Our clients are sophisticated enough to know the virtue of simplicity."

A devotée of French cuisine, Ms. Mulhern travels to France twice a year with her right-hand assistant, Christina Pappajohn, to increase their culinary repertoire. While there, Ms. Mulhern often lectures at La Varenne School of Cooking on the fine art of restaurant management. She also travels to the Napa Valley with the restaurant's wine manager to augment their knowledge of California wines, an integral part of the Garden's large cellar.

Open for lunch and dinner, as well as private parties, the Garden's charming atmosphere and extensive menu invite diners to linger and savor their repast with pleasure.

1617 Spruce Street

### OYSTERS MALPEQUE, WELLFLEET, COTUIT, AND BELON

6 to 8   *oysters per person (Use*
*the different kinds of*
*oysters listed above.)*

*Seaweed*
*2 lemons, cut into wedges*

Wash and scrub the oysters in very cold water. Open just before serving. Serve on the half-shell on a bed of seaweed, garnished by cut lemon baskets or lemon wedges.

*The simplicity of this dish, one of our specialties, is embellished by the use of different kinds of oysters from Prince Edward Island and the Massachusetts coast. The Belon oysters are grown from French seed transplanted to the Maine Coast.*

## ROAST BABY SQUAB ON CROUTONS WITH FOIE GRAS

4 (14-ounce) baby squabs
Salt and pepper to taste
2 teaspoons chopped shallots
4 2" x 3" sheets unsalted
   pork fatback
1 loaf French bread

4 tablespoons butter
FOIE GRAS
½ bunch watercress or
   4 small tomatoes, for
   garnish

1. Preheat oven to 450°.
2. After removing giblets and removing and reserving livers, rub each squab with salt and pepper and ½ teaspoon chopped shallots. Lay sheet of fatback over the breast of each squab.
3. Roast in preheated oven for 15 minutes, or until squab is rosy. Baste with drippings after 8 minutes. While squabs are roasting, sauté slices of French bread in butter until browned to make croutons.
4. Remove squabs from oven and allow to sit for 3 minutes. Cut breasts from each side, keeping each breast in one piece. Detach legs. (Wings may be used if desired.) Arrange the breasts of one squab on a crouton which has been covered with Foie Gras. Place legs on plate. Garnish with watercress or small tomato roses for color. Serve with Celery Root Purée.

*We serve this with a sauce made from a veal stock reduction enriched with butter. The recipe can be found in any classic cookbook. You may also add morels, or dried mushrooms, to give a richness and woodsy taste.*

### FOIE GRAS

Squab livers
2 tablespoons butter
2 ounces foie gras de canard

3 tablespoons Armagnac
Salt to taste

Sauté squab livers in butter for 2 minutes on each side over medium heat. Remove and blend all ingredients by hand until the texture is smooth.

## CELERY ROOT PURÉE

3  cups celery root, peeled
1  cup diced potatoes
1  tablespoon ground shallots

Salt and pepper to taste
3  tablespoons butter

1. Boil celery root in 3 cups water for 5 minutes or until tender. Drain. Boil potatoes in 2 cups of water for 3 minutes or until soft. Drain.
2. Purée celery root and potatoes in food processor with shallots, salt, and pepper. Add butter.
3. Reheat over a medium flame, stirring so the mixture doesn't stick.

*Celery root is just beginning to appear in the markets in this country, although we discovered it in France many years ago. It is a large, brown, tough specimen, but worth the trouble.*

## ENDIVE, WATERCRESS, AND WALNUT SALAD
### with Roquefort Dressing

2  Belgian endives
   ROQUEFORT DRESSING
   (see next page)

1  bunch watercress
½  cup shelled walnut halves

1. Cut endive into 1" pieces. Toss with Roquefort Dressing.
2. Place endive on serving plates. Add watercress sprigs and sprinkle with walnuts.

# THE GARDEN

### ROQUEFORT DRESSING

3 ounces Roquefort cheese
1 cup salad oil
½ cup crème fraîche (see index)
½ cup buttermilk
1 teaspoon fresh black pepper

Salt
Pinch of cayenne
Pinch of white pepper
1 tablespoon chopped parsley
1 tablespoon chopped chives

1. Purée cheese briefly in food processor, being careful not to overbeat.
2. Add oil in a thin stream. Add crème fraîche. Add buttermilk. Stop machine. Add seasonings and herbs and stir.

*If crème fraîche is very thick, add one-eighth cup water. This unique dressing will keep a week in the refrigerator.*

## WHITE CHOCOLATE MOUSSE IN ALMOND BASKETS WITH STRAWBERRY PURÉE

2 cups heavy cream
1 cup sugar
½ cup water
½ cup egg whites (about 4 large)

1 pound white chocolate, cut into small cubes
STRAWBERRY PURÉE
TUILES, or ALMOND BASKETS

1. Whip the cream until stiff. Refrigerate.
2. Heat sugar and water until mixture reaches 250° on a candy thermometer. Meanwhile, beat the egg whites until they form stiff peaks. Add the hot sugar mixture to the egg whites in a slow steady stream and blend for 3 minutes on high speed in an electric mixer.
3. Add the chocolate pieces and beat for 1 more minute at low speed. There should still be some chocolate chunks in the mixture. Remove chilled whipped cream from refrigerator and stir into white chocolate mixture. Chill for 2 hours.
4. When ready to serve, pour Strawberry Purée onto dessert plates. Fill Tuiles with Chocolate Mousse and set into middle of dessert plates.

# THE GARDEN

*The use of white chocolate, the darling of the nouvelle cuisine, is not only aesthetically pleasing, it is also lighter than dark chocolate. Raspberries may be substituted for strawberries when in season. The recipe for the almond cups is an adaptation of one taught by Jean Troisgros at the classes we attended in California at the Mondavi Vineyard.*

### STRAWBERRY PURÉE

| | |
|---|---|
| 2 pints fresh strawberries, cleaned and hulled | 1 tablespoon kirsch |
| 2 to 3 tablespoons sugar, or to taste | |

Purée strawberries in a food processor or mash through a sieve until quite fine. Stir in sugar and kirsch.

### TUILES, or ALMOND BASKETS

| | |
|---|---|
| 4 eggs | ¼ cup all-purpose flour |
| 1 cup sugar | 1 tablespoon butter |
| 1 cup ground or slivered almonds | |

1. Preheat oven to 400°.
2. Mix eggs, sugar, almonds, and flour in a mixing bowl with a spoon until mixture is porous, not smooth. Grease a large flat pan with butter and spoon 3" dollops of batter onto the pan. Spread each mound out with the back of the spoon so it is less than ¼" thick and 4 to 5" in diameter. Bake in preheated oven for 8 to 10 minutes, or until the batter looks brown around the edges.
3. Gently lift each rounded piece off the pan while still warm. Place in small soup cups that are about 4" in diameter. Mold it so that it makes a cup, overlapping edges slightly. Let cool and remove from cups.

*These cookies will keep for two to three days in an airtight container. When pouring dough onto pan, do not worry if there is a hole in it. When cooked, it will spread together.*

# LA GROLLA

*Dinner for Six*

*Peperoni Bagna Caoda*

*Vitello Tonnato*

*Zuppa Valdostana*

*Tortellini Tricolore*

*Faisan à la Crème*

*Salad la Grolla*

*Cannoli*

*Coffee la Grolla*

Wines:
With the Peppers and Soup—Stag's Leap Chardonnay
With the Tortellini and Faisan—Gattinara

*Azan Manjikoff and Giovanni Massaglia, Owners*

*Giovanni Massaglia, Chef*

## *LA GROLLA*

**La** Grolla is a small, intimate restaurant located near Society Hill in an historic site. Originally a taproom in the nineteenth century with gambling in the back room, and then a neighborhood tavern, the owners have restored the original bar in inlaid veneer and maintained an atmosphere of understated charm. Its Italian terra cotta floor, soft colors, and quiet music add to the ambiance.

The choice of a name was difficult. "When you take a Parisian Mongolian and a Northern Italian, how do you choose a name? You pick a word that has the same meaning in both French and Italian. La Grolla literally means a cup of friendship and is used in the Piedmont, Aosta Valley, Savoy, and Provence—the cradles of French and Italian cuisine."

As the owners say, "The bottom line is the food. When you have good atmosphere, good food, and a good place people just come." Chef Giovanni Massaglia specializes in rich Northern Italian cuisine, which he learned as a child in his native country and refined during the ten years he spent as chef on a cruise ship, and later in jobs all over Europe.

Both the owners are very much present at all times and add to the friendly quality of this restaurant. Opened for little more than a year, already they have established a clientele of regular diners as well as those in search of something slightly different in Italian food.

782 South Second Street

### PEPERONI BAGNA CAODA

*This recipe may be made in advance, the peppers and the sauce refrigerated separately, and then combined and reheated on top of the stove.*

| | |
|---|---|
| 6 red bell peppers | 1 cup butter |
| 1 cup garlic cloves, peeled | 1 cup olive oil |
| ½ cup anchovy fillets, drained and halved | ½ cup heavy cream |

1. Roast peppers in a 350° oven for 8 to 10 minutes or until the skins are charred. Remove from oven, peel the skins off and cut the peppers into strips. Set aside.
2. Combine garlic, anchovies, butter, and oil in a small pot. Simmer gently for 30 minutes. Remove from heat and cool to lukewarm. Add heavy cream, return to heat and simmer for 10 minutes.
3. Add peppers to sauce and serve.

*The best way to prepare garlic is to soak it in milk, which removes the bitter aftertaste.*

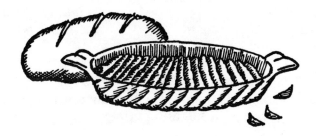

## LA GROLLA

### VITELLO TONNATO

| | |
|---|---|
| 1 small breast of veal | 3 anchovy fillets |
| 1 carrot, chopped | 2 tablespoons capers |
| 1 stalk celery, chopped | 1 can white tuna |
| 2 bay leaves | Parsley sprigs |
| 2 cups HOMEMADE MAYONNAISE | 1 lemon, thinly sliced |

1. Trim the fat and tendons from the veal. Roll up and tie with string or cheesecloth to hold it in shape. Place in a pot with water to cover. Add the carrot, celery, and bay leaves. Bring to a boil; reduce heat and simmer, covered, for 1 hour. Remove the meat and allow to cool.
2. Blend the Mayonnaise, anchovies, 1 tablespoon capers, and the tuna in a blender. The resulting sauce should be slightly thinner in consistency than the mayonnaise.
3. Thinly slice the veal and spread the sauce over the veal slices. Garnish with the remaining capers, parsley, and lemon slices.

*Both the veal and sauce for this cold dish may be prepared in advance and refrigerated.*


### HOMEMADE MAYONNAISE

| | |
|---|---|
| 3 egg yolks | Juice of 1 lemon |
| ½ teaspoon Dijon mustard | Salt and pepper |
| 4 cups olive oil | |

1. Whisk the egg yolks and mustard in a bowl.
2. Slowly add the oil and lemon juice, beating until mayonnaise thickens. Season to taste with salt and pepper.

*This recipe will yield about four cups of mayonnaise. The unused portion may be tightly covered and stored in the refrigerator.*

## LA GROLLA

### ZUPPA VALDOSTANA

*A mixture of veal and chicken stock gives this dish an exceptionally rich taste. Bacon fat may be substituted for olive oil to create a distinctive flavor.*

½ cup olive oil
½ cabbage, cored and sliced
3 medium-size onions, sliced
½ cup flour
1 cup red wine
2 quarts stock, half chicken
 and half veal

1½ teaspoons sage
 Salt and pepper
6 large toasted croutons
½ pound Fontina cheese,
 thinly sliced

1. Heat the oil in a large pot. When it simmers, add the cabbage and onions. Cook 20 minutes, stirring often, until golden brown. Turn the heat to high and stir in the flour, adding more oil if necessary. Allow flour to brown. Add the wine, stock, sage, salt, and pepper. Bring to a boil and simmer for 30 minutes.
2. Pour soup into six crocks. Place a crouton and several thin slices of cheese to cover each crock. Place the crocks under a preheated broiler for 2 to 3 minutes or until the cheese melts.

*For this dish, I recommend only Italian Fontina cheese. Its flavor is unique because the cows that provide the milk for this cheese graze only upon the rare herbs and grasses found in alpine meadows.*

## *LA GROLLA*
### TORTELLINI TRICOLORE

4 eggs
1 egg white
½ (10-ounce) package frozen
  spinach, thawed
6 cups flour
Salt

½ (12-ounce) can red beets
TORTELLINI FILLING
3 cups TOMATO SAUCE
1 cup heavy cream
½ cup grated Parmesan
  cheese

1. Beat the whole eggs and the egg white together.
2. To make green tortellini dough, squeeze all the water from the thawed spinach. Chop finely and add one-third of the egg, 2 cups flour, and a small pinch of salt. Knead until the texture is soft and elastic; set aside.
3. For red tortellini, drain the beets, chop finely, and mix with half the remaining egg, 2 cups flour, and a small pinch of salt. Knead as for green tortellini; set aside.
4. For white tortellini, prepare the remaining egg, 2 cups flour, and a small pinch of salt as above.
5. Roll each batch of dough into an even number of thin sheets, either by hand or in a pasta machine. Dust with flour if the dough is too sticky.
6. Place 1 sheet on a tortellini mold. Press the dough into the mold's indentations.
7. Put the Tortellini Filling in a pastry bag fitted with a #2 plain tip. Pipe filling into each indentation in the dough.
8. Brush a second sheet of the same kind of dough with a little water. Place over the filled first sheet, dampened side down, and press to seal between the pockets. Invert onto a floured surface. Cut the pockets apart with a pasta cutter. Set tortellini aside and repeat process for remaining dough and filling.
9. Place the Tomato Sauce and heavy cream in a large sauté pan. Bring to a simmer; simmer 5 minutes. Add the Parmesan cheese and simmer 3 minutes.
10. Cook the tortellini in a large pot of boiling water for 3 minutes or until al dente. Drain.
11. Place the tortellini in a serving dish, pour the sauce over, and serve.

# LA GROLLA

## TORTELLINI FILLING

1   pound ricotta cheese
1   cup finely chopped walnuts
¼   cup heavy cream

Pinch of nutmeg
Salt and pepper

Blend all ingredients thoroughly in a blender. It may be necessary to add more heavy cream, depending upon the moisture content of the ricotta.

## TOMATO SAUCE

1   cup olive oil
⅔   cup finely chopped carrot
⅔   cup finely chopped celery
⅔   cup finely chopped onion
6   tomatoes, peeled and
     finely chopped

4   cloves garlic, minced
1   tablespoon sugar
4   bay leaves
     Pinch of basil
     Pinch of oregano
     Salt and pepper

1.  Heat the olive oil in a saucepan. Add the carrots, celery, and onion. Simmer over low heat until the onion is golden brown.
2.  Add the remaining ingredients. Return to a boil and simmer 1 hour.

*This sauce may be puréed in a blender after cooking, eliminating the need to finely chop the carrot, celery, onion, and tomatoes.*

### FAISAN A LA CRÈME

1 (3½ to 4-pound) pheasant
½ cup olive oil
1 clove garlic, minced
2 teaspoons chopped rosemary
1 teaspoon sage
1 teaspoon salt
1 teaspoon pepper
½ pound bacon
¾ cup brandy
½ carrot, finely chopped
1 stalk celery, finely chopped
¼ onion, finely chopped
1 teaspoon thyme
4 bay leaves
2 tablespoons flour
2 cups chicken stock
1½ cups heavy cream
½ cup finely chopped filberts, toasted

1. Preheat oven to 350°.
2. Clean the pheasant, removing the giblets. Mix the garlic, rosemary, sage, salt, and pepper with the oil. Brush on and inside the pheasant.
3. Set the bird in a roasting pan on top of several strips of bacon. Cover the top of the pheasant with the remaining bacon. Place the giblets on the side of the roasting pan. Bake in preheated oven for 1 hour, basting frequently with the herb/oil mixture.
4. Remove the pheasant from the pan when done and allow to cool for 10 minutes. Split; remove the breast bones and back bones. Reserve the meat and discard bacon.
5. Glaze the pan juices and giblets by adding ½ cup brandy and heating at a high temperature on top of the stove. Add carrot, celery, onion, thyme, and bay leaves. Simmer, stirring in flour and adding stock until mixture is very thin. Simmer 1 to 1½ hours to reduce and thicken.
6. Strain sauce and transfer to a small pot. Add cream, filberts, and remaining brandy. Warm over low heat.
7. To serve, reheat the pheasant in a shallow pan in a very low oven for 5 to 10 minutes. Divide meat onto serving plates and ladle sauce over.

*This typically Northern Italian dish is usually served with a crouton of polenta on the side. Polenta may be cooked by following the directions on a box of Quaker yellow corn meal, substituting milk for half of the water.*

# LA GROLLA

## SALAD LA GROLLA

1 large head romaine lettuce, cleaned and torn into pieces
2 carrots, thinly sliced

½ cup croutons
¼ cup chopped hazelnuts or walnuts
DRESSING

Toss all ingredients together and top with Dressing.

### SALAD DRESSING

2 cloves garlic, minced
2 shallots, minced
2 anchovy fillets, chopped
½ tablespoon capers

1 egg yolk
1½ cups olive oil
½ cup white wine vinegar
Salt and pepper

Combine ingredients and blend thoroughly.

### CANNOLI

1½ cups bleached flour
1½ teaspoons cocoa powder
1 teaspoon Sanka powder
1½ tablespoons sugar
Pinch of salt
2 tablespoons butter, frozen,
cut into small pieces

1 cup Marsala wine
Oil for deep-frying
FILLING
Confectioners' sugar

1. Put flour, cocoa, Sanka, sugar, salt, and butter in a blender for 20 seconds. Slowly add Marsala. Dough should be slightly elastic; add more flour if loose, or wine if tight.
2. Roll into sheets using a pasta machine. Cut sheets into 5" squares. Roll around hollow cannoli cylinders, sealing the edges with water.
3. Heat oil to 375°. Deep-fry cannoli until golden brown. Remove and put aside until slightly cooled, then slide tubes out. Do not pull or dough will break.
4. Put Filling into pastry bag with a small tip. Squeeze filling into cannoli shells and sprinkle with confectioners' sugar.

#### FILLING

2 pounds ricotta cheese
2 tablespoons orange flower
water

¾ pound semisweet chocolate,
grated
½ cup heavy cream

Blend all ingredients together until smooth.

*The best way to fill the cannoli shells is to insert the pastry tube tip into each shell, withdrawing as you squeeze out the filling.*

### COFFEE LA GROLLA

Per cup:

*1½  ounces Grappa*
*1½  ounces Geneppi*
*1½  ounces hot coffee (made*
*    from a French roast—*
*    mocha and Java)*

*Pinch of sugar*
*Twist of orange*

Combine and serve.

*This rich coffee uses two Northern Italian specialties. Geneppi is a pine liqueur and Grappa is distilled from the dregs of the regional wines. We serve it in the traditional way—in an ornately carved wooden cup made of myrtle with four to six spouts on the sides. It is meant to be passed around the table and shared by the company in good fellowship.*

# HU-NAN

*Dinner for Four*

*Pinwheel Shrimp Rolls*

*Velvet Corn Soup with Crabmeat*

*Chicken Soong with Pine Nuts*

*Boned Bass Provençal*

*Crisp Duck with Five Spice Sauce*

*Mixed Vegetables*

*Ginger Cream*

*Wines:*

*With the Bass—Trapiche Chardonnay, 1977*

*With the Duck—Premiat Pinot Noir, 1978*

*Kan-Chen Foo, Wan Chow Foo, E-Hsin Foo, and Susanna Foo,
Proprietors*

*Susanna Foo, Executive Chef*

# HU-NAN

The Hu-nan is a traditional Chinese restaurant in more than one sense of the word. As E-Hsin Foo says, "My father and mother, Kan-Chen and Wam-Chow Foo, opened the original Hu-nan in 1973 in Wayne. They later moved to Ardmore and the new restaurant was managed by their eldest son, E-ni and his wife, Betty. In 1979, they opened here in Center City and my wife and I manage this Hu-nan. In China, it is a tradition that the family is all-important, and my parents believe that strongly.

"Our cuisine is authentic Hu-nan, far removed from the typical American version of Chinese cooking. We hope to show our patrons that Chinese cuisine is sophisticated and complex, rather than simply a method of stir-frying. Our goal is to be a superb and serious Chinese restaurant."

The decor of Hu-nan is distinctly Oriental and gracious, with a Chinese blue ceiling, touches of gold, and silk bonsai over the bar. It is a perfect location for the three special Chinese dinners given annually by the Foos: the Chinese New Year in January, the Moon Festival in August, and the Dragon Festival in May.

Only two years old, Hu-nan is quickly becoming an institution—a rare setting for those who relish a serious approach to authentic Chinese cuisine.

1721 Chestnut Street

### PINWHEEL SHRIMP ROLLS

*This traditional Hunan recipe demands all fresh ingredients, especially the shrimp.*

| | |
|---|---|
| 5 large eggs | 2 tablespoons vermouth |
| 1 tablespoon salad oil | ¼ cup chicken or fish stock |
| 1 pound raw shrimp, shelled and deveined | 2 tablespoons finely chopped scallions, white part only |
| 2 teaspoons salt | 8 snow peas, diced |
| ⅓ cup fine dried bread crumbs | ½ red sweet pepper or pimiento, diced |
| 1 teaspoon finely minced fresh ginger | 1 small carrot, shredded |
| 1 egg white | OYSTER SAUCE (see next page) |
| ⅛ teaspoon hot pepper powder | |
| ¼ teaspoon white pepper | |

1. Beat the 5 eggs until well-blended. Brush a teflon-lined skillet with half the salad oil. Heat the pan and pour in half the eggs, swirling the pan to let the eggs cover the bottom of the pan. Cook egg "crêpe" until set. Remove from pan and allow to cool. Repeat.
2. Rub the shrimp with 1 teaspoon salt and wash thoroughly under cold running water. Drain shrimp and pat dry. Mince the shrimp with on/off turns of the food processor and transfer to a large mixing bowl. Stir in the remaining salt, the bread crumbs, ginger, egg white, peppers, vermouth, chicken or fish stock, and scallions. Stir vigorously until the mixture is well blended. Add diced snow peas and sweet red pepper or pimiento.
3. Spread half the shrimp mixture on one egg crêpe, top with half of the shredded carrots, and roll up. Repeat with the other crêpe.
4. Place shrimp rolls on a plate in a steamer and steam for 10 minutes. Cool thoroughly and slice on a slant into pieces ⅓" wide. Arrange on a serving plate and serve with Oyster Sauce.

# HU-NAN

## OYSTER SAUCE

¼ cup oyster sauce
¼ cup chicken stock
1 tablespoon soy sauce

1 tablespoon Tabasco sauce
1 teaspoon ground fresh ginger

Mix together, heat in saucepan, and serve warm with Shrimp Rolls.

## VELVET CORN SOUP WITH CRABMEAT

*The sweet corn and the crabmeat make an unusually good combination. This recipe is an adaptation of Chinese cuisine with touches of the West added to it.*

4 large fresh ears of corn (8 ounces of frozen corn may be substituted if necessary, seasonally)
1 quart chicken stock
Salt
1 teaspoon white pepper
1 teaspoon fresh ground ginger

1 tablespoon cornstarch dissolved in 2 tablespoons cold water
2 egg whites, beaten
8 ounces crabmeat
1 scallion, chopped

1. Using a sharp knife, slice the kernels of fresh corn from their cobs into a bowl, being careful not to cut too deeply into the cob. Put in a food processor and grind fine.
2. Place the chicken stock in a saucepan and bring to a boil. Add the corn, salt, white pepper, and fresh ginger, stirring constantly. Bring to a boil again. Turn to a low heat and cook for 5 minutes. Pour in the cornstarch mixture. Stir constantly until the soup has thickened and become clear. Immediately pour in the egg whites, still stirring. Add crabmeat.
3. Turn off the heat and quickly pour the hot soup into a tureen and Sprinkle with chopped scallions.

### CHICKEN SOONG WITH PINE NUTS

*The lettuce and vegetables are very crispy, giving this finger food a crunchy taste. This may be used as an hors d'oeuvres.*

| | |
|---|---|
| 1 head lettuce | ⅓ cup diced water chestnuts |
| 8 ounces boned chicken breast, finely shredded | ⅓ cup diced Chinese black mushrooms |
| ½ teaspoon salt | ⅓ cup diced carrots |
| 1 teaspoon cornstarch | ⅓ cup pine nuts, roasted |
| 4⅓ tablespoons cooking oil | 2 tablespoons soy sauce |
| 1 teaspoon freshly ground ginger | 1 tablespoon rice wine |
| 1 teaspoon minced garlic | 1 tablespoon vinegar |
| | ¼ cup hoisin sauce |

1. Break off and wash whole lettuce leaves, arranging as cups on platter.
2. Marinate shredded chicken with salt, cornstarch, and 1 teaspoon cooking oil for 15 minutes.
3. Heat 4 tablespoons of oil in a wok to 350° to 375°. Add the chicken and stir-fry for 2 minutes until the chicken turns firm and white. Remove the chicken from the wok and put in a dish.
3. Add ginger and garlic to the wok. Then add water chestnuts, Chinese mushrooms, and carrots and stir-fry for a couple of minutes. Pour chicken and pine nuts into the wok. Add soy sauce, rice wine, and vinegar. Stir-fry quickly over high heat.
4. To serve, place one lettuce leaf on a plate and add a rounded tablespoon of the chicken mixture. Top with 1 teaspoon of hoisin sauce. Fold the lettuce over and eat with fingers.

*The chicken filling may be made in advance and refrigerated. This dish may also be served cold.*

### BONED BASS PROVENÇAL

*French touches, such as the boning of the fish, have been added to this traditional Shanghai dish to make it an interesting mélange of East and West.*

| | |
|---|---|
| 1 whole sea bass (about 2 pounds), cleaned and scaled | 2 tablespoons soy sauce |
| 1 teaspoon salt | 3 to 4 cups cooking oil |
| ½ teaspoon white pepper | 1 scallion, finely shredded |
| ½ cup flour | 1 fresh hot pepper, finely shredded |
| 2 cups chicken stock | 4 slices ginger, finely shredded |
| 4 tablespoons vinegar | 2 tablespoons cornstarch dissolved in 2 tablespoons of water |
| 4 tablespoons sugar | |
| 2 tablespoons vermouth | |
| 1 tablespoon minced fresh garlic | |
| ¼ teaspoon dry hot pepper flakes | |

1. Wash the bass. With a sharp knife, remove the head. Lay the fish on its side and split in half, cutting along the backbone without removing the tail. Score the flesh side of each fillet and sprinkle with salt and white pepper mixed together. Roll in flour. Coat the head with flour, too.
2. Combine chicken stock, vinegar, sugar, vermouth, garlic, hot pepper flakes, and soy sauce in a separate bowl and set aside.
3. Heat cooking oil deep enough to cover fish in a deep fryer to 350°. Holding the fish by the tail, lower it into the hot oil. Then put in the head and fry both for 7 to 10 minutes. Lift the fish out, drain the oil, and place the fish on a heated platter with the head in its original position. Decorate with scallions, fresh hot pepper, and ginger.
4. Pour chicken stock mixture into a skillet and bring to a boil. Add the cornstarch mixture and cook until it thickens for another minute. Pour sauce over fish and serve immediately.

## CRISP DUCK WITH FIVE SPICE SAUCE

*This is a traditional Hu-nan dish. In China, duck is always served for special occasions and each region has its own special ways of preparing it.*

| | |
|---|---|
| 1 young duckling, about 4½ to 5½ pounds | 1 tablespoon salt |
| 4 quarts water | 1 cup dark soy sauce |
| 2 tablespoons five spice powder | 3 scallions, cut in half |
| | 1 cup vermouth |
| 4 slices fresh ginger | BATTER |
| 3 cloves garlic, crushed | SAUCE (see next page) |
| | 4 cups cooking oil |

1. Combine water, five spice, ginger, garlic, salt, soy sauce, scallions, and vermouth into a large pot. Bring to a vigorous boil and slowly insert duck. Bring liquid and duck to a boil again and immediately turn heat to low. Simmer, covered, for 1½ hours. Remove duck from liquid and let cool, reserving stock for use in Sauce.
2. Cut the duck in half and remove bones.
3. Brush Batter over duck halves and allow to dry.
4. Heat enough oil to cover duck to 350° to 375°. Carefully slip the duck halves into the oil. Fry for 3 to 5 minutes or until golden brown and crisp. Remove from oil and drain on absorbent paper.
5. Cut duck into manageable strips and arrange on platter. Serve with Sauce.

### BATTER

| | |
|---|---|
| 3 tablespoons water chestnut flour | 2 tablespoons white wine |
| 1 tablespoon vinegar | ⅛ teaspoon salt |
| | ⅛ teaspoon red pepper powder |

Mix all ingredients together.

# HU-NAN

### SAUCE

½ cup duck stock
½ cup chicken stock
1 teaspoon cornstarch dissolved in 1 tablespoon water

2 tablespoons Grand Marnier
1 scallion, finely shredded

1. Pour duck and chicken stocks into heated saucepan. Bring to a boil and add cornstarch mixture. Cook, stirring constantly, until sauce thickens.
2. Turn off heat and add Grand Marnier and scallion.

## MIXED VEGETABLES

*The secret of good Chinese vegetables is the freshness of the ingredients and the care taken never to overcook.*

2 tablespoons cooking oil
1 teaspoon finely minced fresh garlic
¼ cup Chinese black mushrooms
¼ cup bok choy stems, cut into 1" pieces
¼ cup water chestnuts
¼ cup baby corn

¼ cup red sweet pepper, cut into 1" pieces
¼ cup sliced bamboo shoots
½ cup snow peas
1 teaspoon salt
1 tablespoon soy sauce
¼ cup chicken stock
1 teaspoon cornstarch dissolved in 1 tablespoon water

1. Heat the oil in a wok to 350° and add the garlic and black mushrooms. Stir-fry for a few seconds. Add bok choy, water chestnuts, baby corn, red pepper, bamboo shoots, and snow peas and stir-fry for 2 minutes. Add salt, soy sauce, and chicken stock. Cook until mixture starts to boil.
2. Add cornstarch mixture and stir until thickened. Transfer to a plate and serve.

### GINGER CREAM

*This recipe was provided by our dear friend, Mrs. Hermie Kranzdorf, who has written several cookbooks. With her help, we created this unique blend of Chinese and French cuisine.*

2 cups half and half
1 package gelatin
1 teaspoon fresh squeezed ginger juice, or ½ teaspoon powdered ginger
½ cup sugar
Dash of salt

2 egg yolks
1 tablespoon preserved ginger, diced very fine
1 cup heavy cream, whipped
Mandarin orange segments or lychee for garnish

1. Pour the half and half into a saucepan and sprinkle the gelatin over the top. Let sit for a few minutes to soften.
2. Add ginger juice, sugar, and salt. Stir in the egg yolks. Heat the custard, stirring constantly over medium heat for about 5 minutes or until it thickens enough to coat the back of the spoon.
3. Strain the custard into a bowl. Chill until it begins to harden, approximately one hour.
4. Stir the diced ginger into the custard and fold in the whipped cream. Pour into 6 serving dishes. Chill until set for approximately 2 hours.
5. Serve with mandarin oranges or lychee.

*Dinner for Six*

*Terrine de Ris de Veau aux Légumes*

*Consommé au Fumet du Thym Citronne*

*Cailles Grillés avec la Compote de Poires et de Pommes*

*Raisins Frites*

*Pois Mange-Tout*

*Tarte aux Poires*

*Wine:*

*Grand Crú Vineyards Gewürztraminer*

*Anita Pignataro and Alphonse Pignataro, Owners*
*Alphonse Pignataro, Chef*

**M**organ's reflects the strong personal enthusiasm of its owners, Anita and Alphonse Pignataro. It is an unusual restaurant with the romantic and intimate ambiance of a delightful country inn. Morgan's changes its menu completely every ten weeks. As Alphonse Pignataro says, "It's always an exciting challenge to create and cook new menu items and as a result, our level of interest is kept quite high. In addition, our regular clients seem to share our excitement." Morgan's also orchestrates four very special dinners each year, complete with wines for each course. Anita Pignataro says, "Although we send invitations to all of our customers, it is often the same ones who return for each dinner, creating an atmosphere of conviviality and friendship."

Alphonse describes his cuisine as "personal and subtle, inspired by the foods of France and Northern Italy." Although he is unusually creative, he prides himself upon the fact that " . . . our restaurant is very successful and honest. We sensibly combine the finest quality of ingredients and prepare them so as to maintain their integrity."

He describes his entrance into the restaurant business as a "classic fantasy come true." He was a teacher and a Sunday cook who dreamed, with his wife, of owning a restaurant. After running two restaurants, the opportunity arose to purchase Morgan's in 1976. Alphonse says, "Anita and I feel we have created precisely the type of restaurant we wanted and we derive a great deal of enjoyment and satisfaction from our proprietorship." The Pignataro's spirit of élan and devotion to creative cuisine have made Morgan's a very special place to dine, in a pleasantly relaxed setting.

135 South 24th Street

### TERRINE DE RIS DE VEAU AUX LÉGUMES

*This terrine may be kept for a couple of weeks in the refrigerator, or it may be frozen.*

| | |
|---|---|
| ½ pound pork fat | 2 eggs |
| 3 cloves garlic | ½ pound spinach |
| 2 pounds ground veal | 2 carrots |
| ½ cup brandy | 2 parsnips |
| ½ cup cream | ½ pound green beans |
| Pinch of allspice | 1 pound bacon |
| 1 teaspoon thyme | SWEETBREADS (see next |
| 2 teaspoons salt | page) |
| 1 teaspoon white pepper | Olives |
| ¼ cup flour | Cornichons |

1. Purée garlic and pork fat in food processor. Add and combine veal, brandy, cream, allspice, thyme, salt, white pepper, flour, and eggs.
2. Clean and then blanch spinach by pouring boiling water over it. Peel carrots and parsnips, julienne and steam for 2 to 4 minutes or until tender. Snip the ends of the green beans and steam for 2 to 4 minutes.
3. Preheat oven to 325°. Line an 8-cup loaf pan (9" × 5" × 3") with bacon, pressing strips on bottom, along the sides, and at the ends, with the excess hanging over the edge of the pan to be folded over the top later.
4. Pack one-fourth of the forcemeat into the pan, carefully pushing it into the corners and patting to avoid any air holes. Place one-half of the carrots, parsnips and green beans on the forcemeat to create a second layer. Arrange them in separate rows, alternating colors. Pack another one-fourth of the forcemeat into the pan. Wrap spinach around Sweetbreads and place a row of them in the center of the pan. Pack another one-fourth of the forcemeat around and above the Sweetbreads. Place the remaining vegetables in the next layer as above. Pack the remaining forcemeat on top. Fold bacon strips over top.

(continued on next page)

5. Seal pan tightly with foil. Set in a larger shallow pan filled with enough hot water to come halfway up the side of the loaf pan. Place in preheated oven and cook for about 1 hour. Test the terrine by inserting a knife into the center of the loaf. If the tip is warm, the terrine is done.

6. Remove from oven and loosen foil. Do not pour off juices. Weight the loaf with a brick to press out the fat and make the loaf firm for slicing. When the terrine has come to room temperature, refrigerate overnight.

7. In the morning, remove weight and foil. Unmold by running a knife around the edge and holding pan briefly in a basin of water. Invert onto a cold platter. Serve in slices with olives and cornichons.

### SWEETBREADS

| | |
|---|---|
| 1 pound sweetbreads | 2 cloves |
| 2 tablespoons flour | |

1. Place sweetbreads in cold water for several hours, changing the water frequently.
2. Put sweetbreads in a saucepan with water to cover and add flour and cloves. Bring to a boil and then gently simmer for 15 minutes.
3. Place under cold water until meat is cold. Pull off the sinews—the rubbery pieces that adhere to the meat—and remove as much of the membrane as possible.

*The recipe for this terrine was developed at Morgan's. The nicest thing about it is that it's so pretty. When it's done, you have created something really beautiful.*

### CONSOMMÉ AU FUMET DU THYM CITRONNE

*For this recipe, it is essential to use fresh lemon thyme. This can be purchased through a local greenhouse if not available at your market.*

| | |
|---|---|
| 2½ quarts VEAL STOCK | Salt and pepper |
| 5 ripe tomatoes | 4 egg whites |
| 12 sprigs lemon thyme | 4 egg shells |

1. Place 4 tomatoes and Veal Stock in large pot. Add 6 sprigs of lemon thyme and salt and pepper to taste. Cook for 1 hour, or until the flavor of tomato and thyme have permeated the stock. Strain stock.
2. Clarify stock by lightly beating egg whites and egg shells together. Put consommé and egg mixture into pot and bring to a boil. The eggs will form a raft on the top of the pot. When the consommé looks clear, remove eggs. Pour consommé into strainer lined with cheesecloth. Repeat until consommé is perfectly clear.
3. Blanch remaining tomato by submerging it in hot water to loosen skin. Peel off skin and remove seeds, leaving only pulp. Dice.
4. Pour soup into bowls. Garnish with diced tomato and sprigs of lemon thyme.

### VEAL STOCK

| | |
|---|---|
| 3 pounds veal knuckles and veal bones | 3 large leeks |
| 3 cloves | 1 celery rib |
| 1½ large onions | A sprinkle of vegetable oil |
| 3 large carrots | Large BOUQUET GARNI |
| | 3 quarts cold water |

1. Preheat oven to 400°. Put cloves in onion and add to veal, carrots, leeks, and celery in roasting pan. Sprinkle vegetable oil on top. Cook for about 40 minutes, or until the bones are well caramelized.
2. Put mixture in large pot on top of the stove. Add Bouquet Garni and water and simmer, uncovered, over very low flame for 6 to 8 hours. Skim the top as it cooks. If the level of water gets too low to yield 2½ quarts of stock, add more, sparingly.
3. Strain.

*This creates a nice, strong-tasting stock. Frozen veal base or bouillon cubes may be used instead of the above recipe, but the taste will not be the same. Veal stock may be cooked early in the week and refrigerated until needed.*

### BOUQUET GARNI

| | |
|---|---|
| 8 sprigs fresh parsley | 1 tablespoon thyme |
| 4 bay leaves | 15 black peppercorns |

Tie up in cheesecloth.

## CAILLES GRILLÉS AVEC LA COMPOTE
## DE POIRES ET DE POMMES

*This is best if cooked over hickory chips.*

| | |
|---|---|
| 12 quail | *COMPOTE DE POIRES* |
| 3 tablespoons sweet butter, melted | *ET DE POMMES* |
| | *RAISINS FRITES* |

1. Split quail with knife or poultry shears. Remove back and neck bones. Brush quail with melted butter.
2. Cook over coals on a very hot fire. Start with the breast side down. Cook 3 to 5 minutes or until golden brown. Flip over and cook 3 to 5 minutes on the other side. Meat should be kept as pink as possible. Serve with Compote de Poires et de Pommes and Raisins Frites.

*This dish is simply elegant. The secret is not to overcook the quail as it will lose its delicate taste.*

### COMPOTE DE POIRES ET DE POMMES

| | |
|---|---|
| 6 cups peeled, cored and chopped apples | 1 pound brown sugar |
| 6 cups peeled, cored, and chopped pears | 1½ cups white vinegar |
| 1 cup pitted and chopped dates | 2 teaspoons salt |
| 1 cup chopped olives | ½ teaspoon chopped fresh ginger |
| 1 cup chopped onions | ½ teaspoon toasted and ground coriander seeds |
| ½ cup green peppers | ½ teaspoon allspice |

1. In a large kettle, combine all ingredients except ginger, coriander, and allspice. Tie spices in a cheesecloth and add.
2. Bring mixture to a boil. Cook slowly, stirring frequently, for 1 hour or until mixture is thickened. Remove spice bag and refrigerate compote.

*The beauty of this recipe is that it can be made well in advance as it will keep for at least two weeks. The yield is about 12 cups and it can be served with many dishes or processed for bottling.*

### RAISINS FRITES

| | |
|---|---|
| 1 cup flour | 1 pound seedless grapes, |
| ¾ cup beer | white or red |
| ½ teaspoon salt | Vegetable oil |

1. Mix flour, beer and salt in the mixer until smooth.
2. Break grapes into 6 bunches.
3. Fill a 2-quart saucepan or deep fryer halfway to the top with vegetable oil. Heat oil until it is almost smoking.
4. Coat grapes with batter by dipping into bowl. Make sure each grape is lightly coated. Immediately after coating each bunch of grapes, place gently into cooking oil with slotted spoon. Allow to cook about 30 seconds, or until grapes brown slightly. Place on paper towels to drain and repeat with each bunch of grapes. Serve.

*Be sure not to fill the fryer more than half full of oil or it will spatter. The oil should be hot enough so that the batter will cook and the grapes will not.*


## POIS MANGE-TOUT

| | |
|---|---|
| 1 pound snow peas | Salt |
| 3 tablespoons sweet butter | |

1. Snap off snow pea stems and rinse.
2. Cover ¼" of the bottom of the sauté pan with water. Add butter and salt. Add snow peas and cook over high flame, constantly moving pan. Cook no longer than 5 to 7 minutes. If necessary, drain. Serve.

*Ideally, the water will boil off and only the butter will remain when the snow peas are finished cooking. This is an alternative to steaming and will produce crisp, fresh-tasting snow peas.*

## TARTE AUX POIRES

| | |
|---|---|
| *PASTRY* | *1 clove* |
| *PASTRY CREAM* | *1 cinnamon stick* |
| *FRANGIPANE* | *½ lemon* |
| *5 slightly under-ripe Bosc pears* | *Burgundy or other red wine* |
| *¾ cup sugar* | *½ cup red currant jam* |

1. Prepare Pastry, Pastry Cream and Frangipane.
2. Peel and core pears, leaving whole. Place sugar, clove, cinnamon, lemon and equal parts wine and water to cover pears in a large pot. Bring to boil, stirring until sugar is dissolved. Lower temperature and add pears. Poach until barely soft, about 20 minutes. Remove pears and allow to drain.
3. Preheat oven to 350°.
4. Blend Pastry Cream with Frangipane and pour into crust.
5. Halve 4 of the pears lengthwise. Arrange pears in pie shell so that each half will become one piece of pie when it is sliced. Push slightly as you set pears in the filling, making sure that the filling covers the sides of the pears. Thinly slice the remaining pear. Arrange pieces so that they create a "flower" in the middle of the tart.
6. Set the tart in the oven. Cook 35 to 40 minutes, or until filling is "set" and the crust is a golden brown. Remove from oven.
9. While tart is cooking, prepare glaze by melting jam in a saucepan. Allow to cook 3 to 4 minutes. Strain.
8. Brush glaze on top of tart while it is still warm and serve.

### PASTRY

| | |
|---|---|
| *3 cups flour* | *1 whole egg* |
| *Pinch of salt* | *1 egg yolk* |
| *6 tablespoons sugar* | *½ pound sweet butter, cut into cubes* |
| *Zest of 1 lemon* | |

1. Combine flour, salt, sugar and lemon zest.
2. In a measuring cup, combine egg, egg yolk, and enough water to make ½ cup of liquid.

3. Working quickly, knead butter into dry ingredients with fingertips until it has the consistency of oatmeal. Add liquid and blend with fingers until dough comes together in a ball. Break dough by pushing it into small pieces with the heel of the hand and gathering together again to form a ball. Wrap in waxed paper and refrigerate for 1 hour.

4. Roll dough out to fit into a 9" tart pan. Let it rest in the refrigerator again for ½ hour.

5. Preheat oven to 350°. Line shell with aluminum foil and place rice or beans inside tart pan to weight the crust down so it will not rise during baking. Cook for 10 to 15 minutes, or until lightly browned. Remove from oven and allow to cool.

### PASTRY CREAM

| | |
|---|---|
| 1 cup half and half | 2 tablespoons flour |
| ¼ cup granulated sugar | ½ tablespoon rum |
| 3 egg yolks | |

1. Place half and half in saucepan and bring to a boil. Remove from heat.

2. Combine egg yolks and sugar and add to half and half. Beat with a wire whisk until mixture thickens and forms a yellow ribbon when whisk is lifted.

3. Gently stir in flour and add rum. Bring to boil, stirring constantly with whisk. Allow to cool in pot.

### FRANGIPANE

| | |
|---|---|
| ¼ pound sweet butter | 1 cup ground almonds |
| 1 cup powdered sugar | 2 eggs |

Combine butter and sugar in mixer. Add almonds and eggs and beat until it forms a ribbon when beater is lifted.

*This tart may be served hot or cold. The pastry, pears, and filling may be made in advance and stored in the refrigerator. If there is excess dough and filling, it may be reserved for later use, to be filled with poached apples or peaches, following the procedure described above.*

# sannas

*Dinner for Four*

*Ty's Tangy Tomato Soup*

*Lobster Henrietta*

*Hearts and Stars Salad*

*Poisson Chinoise*

*Double Chocolate Mousse Cake*

*Wines:*

*With the Soup and Lobster—Foppiano Dry Chenin Blanc, 1980*

*With the Poisson—Jekel Vineyards Chardonnay, 1979*

*With the Cake—A. Charbaut et Fils, Champagne Blanc de Blancs, 1973*

*Sanna and David Cohen, Owners*

*Larry Bellinger, Chef*

Sannas, housed in the site of a former bank, is a very recent addition to the Philadelphia restaurant scene. Already awarded three stars by *Philadelphia Magazine*, its youthful and enthusiastic crew—from co-owner Sanna, the creative chef, and her brother, David, a film-maker, to Suchart, the working chef, and the architect and builders who renovated the historical site—together contribute to make Sannas innovative and experimental.

Sanna, who began her professional career at the Fishmarket and the Frög, describes her eclectic cuisine as "a little of this and a little of that—things that taste good together." She is careful to combine foods that also look well together because "presentation is an integral and essential part of all food preparation."

Both she and her brother credit their interest in cooking to their mother. Sanna says, "As a family, we spent our lives in the kitchen, having fun and experimenting. Even today, many of our most successful recipes are adaptations of my mother's." Sanna's favorites are the desserts. "Dessert is, for me," she says, "the most important part of the meal." As a result, the menu always offers from nine to fifteen lavish desserts, in addition to homemade ice cream and sorbet. New selections are added each week.

The decor of Sannas, a soft blending of art deco and hi-tech, is relaxed and comfortable. Some of the original features of the building have been maintained, such as the old brick wall and the vault door which now works perfectly, Sanna says "as our refrigerator door." This unusual setting is uniquely suited for the live jazz concerts staged at Sannas each week. Whether interested in a full course dinner, a late evening snack, or a special holiday meal, a diner is sure to be delighted with the warm ambiance of Sannas.

239 Chestnut Street

## TY'S TANGY TOMATO SOUP

*This recipe was derived from a soup made for Ty Bailey (owner of the Knave of Hearts). We use it as a substitute for chicken soup—and it seems to have the same magical curative powers.*

1 large, boned chicken breast
4 tablespoons unsalted butter
½ medium-size onion, thinly sliced
1 large carrot, thinly sliced
1 stalk celery, thinly sliced
1 tablespoon oregano Salt, black pepper, garlic to taste
1 (1-pound) can whole peeled tomatoes

1 (1-pound) can tomato purée
1 cup chicken stock
2 ounces cheddar cheese, grated
2 ounces Jarlsberg cheese, grated
4 tablespoons grated Parmesan cheese
½ cup herb croutons

1. Sauté chicken breast in 1 tablespoon butter for about 5 minutes. Remove and cut into cubes.
2. In a large pot, sauté onion, carrot, celery, oregano, salt, pepper and garlic in remaining butter for about 6 minutes or until vegetables soften. Add tomatoes and tomato purée. Simmer on low heat for 10 to 15 minutes.
3. Add chicken stock and cubed chicken breast. Add cheeses and simmer until melted. Garnish with croutons.

## LOBSTER HENRIETTA

*The spring roll wrappers are available in Oriental food markets.*

16 (2" by 2") spring roll
   wrappers
1 pound cooked and
   shredded fresh lobster meat

1 egg yolk
3 cups peanut oil
   HENRIETTA SAUCE

1. Fill spring roll wrappers with lobster meat. Roll on the diagonal, pressing ends in to form a package. Hold together with a dot of egg yolk.
2. Deep-fry in very hot peanut oil (375°) for a few minutes until light brown on the edges.
3. Serve with Henrietta Sauce.

### HENRIETTA SAUCE

¼ cup Dessaux Fils wine
   vinegar
2 cloves garlic, peeled and
   finely chopped
3 tablespoons wine vinegar

2 tablespoons sugar
¼ cup grated carrot
¼ teaspoon red pepper flakes
   Black pepper to taste

Mix all ingredients together.

*Henrietta Sauce is a traditional Thai recipe which has been handed down in the family of a close friend who then modernized it with Sanna.*

### HEARTS AND STARS SALAD

*This salad was created to revivify the typical hearts of palm. The vinaigrette is a versatile marinade which may be used to marinate fish and meat.*

| | |
|---|---|
| 1 head red leaf lettuce | ½ Bermuda onion, sliced |
| 4 hearts of palm | ½ cup crumbled feta cheese |
| 1 cucumber, sliced | VINAIGRETTE |
| 1 tomato, sliced | |

1. Wash and prepare lettuce. Arrange leaves on individual plates. Place hearts of palm in the center of lettuce. Around the hearts of palm, place a few cucumber slices, tomatoes, and one slice of onion. Top palms with feta cheese.
2. Drizzle Vinaigrette on salad.

#### VINAIGRETTE

| | |
|---|---|
| 3 tablespoons lemon juice | 2 tablespoons Dijon mustard |
| 1 teaspoon red wine vinegar | A few pinches of pepper |
| 2 tablespoons heavy cream | Small pinch of salt |
| 3 tablespoons olive oil | 2 cloves garlic, chopped |
| 5 tablespoons vegetable oil | |

Whisk ingredients together in the order listed.

### POISSON CHINOISE

*This is one of the few items on our menu that contains no butter, cream, or oil. If the fish is not marinated, this is also perfect for people on a low salt diet. For home use, a vegetable steamer may be used instead of the four Chinese steamers. The advantage of the Chinese steamers is their attractive presentation.*

| | |
|---|---|
| 1 pound red snapper fillets | 1 zucchini, julienned |
| 4 ounces sole | 1 green pepper, julienned |
| MARINADE | 8 ears baby corn |
| ½ head red cabbage, washed and separated | ½ pound straw mushrooms, left whole and washed |
| 1 large carrot, julienned | BLACK BEAN SAUCE |

1. Marinate fish in Marinade for 1 hour at room temperature.
2. In each of four Chinese steamers, place a layer of red cabbage on the bottom. In the center, place the marinated fish, arranging carrots, zucchini, and green pepper around them. Add 2 ears of baby corn and a few straw mushrooms to each basket and close.
3. Steam baskets over simmering water for approximately 15 minutes. Serve with Black Bean Sauce.

### *MARINADE*

1½  cups mushroom soy sauce
½  cup white wine

4  tablespoons chopped garlic
2  tablespoons white pepper

Combine all ingredients.

### *BLACK BEAN SAUCE*

¼  cup black bean sauce
1  tablespoon hoisin sauce

1  tablespoon lemon juice

Mix all ingredients well.

*The black bean sauce and hoisin sauce may be purchased at Oriental markets.*

## SANNAS

### DOUBLE CHOCOLATE MOUSSE CAKE

*This cake serves twenty. However, it may be frozen without the icing. After it is cut, it will last four days if covered tightly. This provides a nice rich finale to a light dinner.*

| | |
|---|---|
| 7  extra-large eggs | ½  cup Hershey's cocoa powder |
| 1  cup sugar | ¼  pound sweet butter, melted |
| ¼  teaspoon salt | MOUSSE FILLING |
|     Dash of vanilla | FROSTING |
| ½  cup flour | |

1. Put uncracked eggs in a stainless steel bowl with hot water to cover. Allow to sit for 10 minutes to warm.
2. Preheat oven to 350°.
3. Break eggs into mixing bowl. Using whisk attachment to mixer, whip, adding sugar, salt, and vanilla. Continue whipping until tripled in volume.
4. Fold in sifted flour and cocoa. Fold in melted butter half at a time.
5. Pour cake mixture (genoise) into an 11″ by 15″ cake pan lined with waxed paper which has been lightly greased with butter or shortening. Bake in preheated oven for 23 minutes. When cake is done, it will be springy and will have pulled away a little from the edges of the pan. Cool on rack.
6. Remove the bottom of a 9″ spring-form pan. Cut genoise to the size of pan bottom. Split the circle in half horizontally, so that you now have a bottom and top for the cake. Take the remaining piece of cake and cut into 3 pieces. Put the bottom circle of genoise into pan. Line the sides with three strips you have just cut. Fill with Mousse Filling. Put other circle on top. Cover and refrigerate for at least 5 hours. Remove by placing plate on top and inverting.
7. Cover cake with frosting. Use a #9 pastry bag with a star point to create a decorative edge.

# SANNAS

### MOUSSE FILLING

1½ pounds sweet chocolate  
1 cup brewed coffee  
½ cup honey  

4 eggs  
3 cups heavy cream  
Pinch of salt

1. Melt chocolate and coffee in double boiler over simmering water, adding honey when the chocolate is melted. Remove from heat. Whisk until cool.
2. Separate eggs. Whisk yolks into chocolate. In a separate bowl whip egg whites and salt until mixture is stiff, not dry—forming soft peaks. Fold into chocolate gently. Whip cream and fold in. Cover and refrigerate.

*Be careful to fold in chocolate gently. If not—you may end up with chocolate soup that will not harden. A few more egg whites will bring it back if this happens.*

### FROSTING

2 cups heavy cream  
¼ cup confectioners' sugar  

¼ teaspoon vanilla

Whip ingredients together.

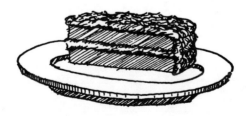

# Tang's

*Dinner for Four*


*Hot and Sour Soup*

*Spring Rolls*

*Szechuan Shrimp*

*Crispy Duckling with Vegetables*

*Fried Rice*

*Seasonal Fruit*

*Tea*

*Wine:*

*Saké*


*Philip Tang, Proprietor and Chef*

## TANG'S

Tang's is considered by owner Philip Tang to be "a Chinese restaurant for the connoisseur of Chinese food." He says, "I consider myself a purist. I refuse to serve food that is not authentic and traditional. Our guests use chopsticks and are offered their choice of Szechuan, Cantonese, Shanghai, or Mandarin cuisine. We do not offer salt, pepper, or sugar at the table and we serve none of the so-called Chinese dishes, such as chow mein, chop suey, or fortune cookies. I refuse to compromise my belief that the American palate is adventuresome and sophisticated enough to appreciate the excellence of true Chinese cuisine.

"The requisites of superb Chinese cooking," continues Philip, "are listed in the following sequence: one, presentation; two, smell; three, taste. Each is equally important; ideally, the first two should prepare the diner for the delightful taste of his repast."

The simple and casually chic decor of Tang's creates an ambiance for the meal to follow. While the bright red paper lanterns and the scrolls on the wall set an unmistakably Chinese note, the mood is easy and not overly ethnic. The dinner is served on charmingly painted china—as Philip says, "from China"—and each table is decorated with a delicate vase of fresh flowers.

Philip Tang, originally from mainland China and Hong Kong, has been in the United States since 1969. He trained under his brother, who owns the Mayflower in Chinatown, and decided to open Tang's three years ago "so that I could fulfill my dream of preparing and serving food in the traditional style."

His most memorable dinner was one he prepared to order for a group of forty Chinese scientists who were visiting Philadelphia. "The meal," he says, "consisted of ten courses; and afterwards, my compatriots insisted on coming back to the kitchen to congratulate me personally." For the serious aficionado of Chinese food, Tang's offers an excellent chance to sample the cuisine from different areas in China, in a relaxed and understated setting.

429 South Street

# TANG'S

## HOT AND SOUR SOUP

2 dried wood ears
10 dried tiger lily buds
6 cups chicken broth
1 teaspoon salt
2 ounces fresh mushrooms, sliced
2 ounces straw mushrooms
2 water chestnuts, sliced
⅓ cup bamboo shoots, shredded

1 square bean curd, drained and shredded
¼ pound chicken meat, shredded
2 tablespoons vinegar
2 tablespoons hot sauce
½ teaspoon white pepper
¼ cup cornstarch
1 egg, beaten
1 tablespoon sesame oil

1. Soak wood ears and tiger lily buds in 2 cups of hot water for 10 minutes to soften. Remove from water and shred.
2. Combine chicken broth, salt, and all vegetables, including wood ears, tiger lily buds, and bean curd in a saucepan. Bring to a boil over high heat and then reduce heat to medium. Add chicken shreds, vinegar, hot sauce, and white pepper.
3. Dissolve cornstarch in 6 tablespoons of water to make a paste. Bring soup back to a boil and slowly stir in the paste. Return to medium heat. Stir in egg and sesame oil and serve.

*This hot and spicy Szechuan soup is an excellent and hearty beginning for the meal.*

## SPRING ROLLS

6 cups plus 3 tablespoons
   peanut or vegetable oil
1 cup bean sprouts
¼ pound chicken meat,
   shredded
2 ounces fresh mushrooms,
   sliced
2 water chestnuts, sliced

¼ cup bamboo shoots
1 tablespoon oyster sauce
¼ cup chicken broth
¼ teaspoon salt
   Dash of pepper
   Dash of sesame oil
4 spring roll skins

1. Add 1 tablespoon of oil to the wok and bring to high heat. Pour in bean sprouts and stir-fry for 1 minute. Place cooked bean sprouts in a drainer to remove excess water.
2. Clean wok and add 2 tablespoons of oil. Bring to high heat and add chicken. Stir-fry for 1 minute and add mushrooms, water chestnuts, and bamboo shoots. Stir-fry for half a minute. Add oyster sauce, chicken broth, salt, pepper, and sesame oil. Mix well. Remove from heat and let cool for 15 minutes.
3. Place 1 spring roll skin on a flat surface with the corner at the top. Place ¼ portion of the cooked bean sprouts below the center of the skin. Add ¼ portion of the chicken filling on top. Place the bottom corner of the skin over the filling and roll over once. Fold the right and left corners into the center and continue rolling toward top corner. Repeat with remaining spring rolls and filling.
4. Pour 6 cups of oil into the cleaned wok and bring it to 325°. Slowly place the spring rolls into the oil. Cook until they turn brown. Serve immediately.

*When filling the spring roll, it may be "glued" with a dab of egg. This typical Shang'hai dish should be served with hot Chinese mustard.*

### SZECHUAN SHRIMP

½ pound (21 to 25) medium
shrimp, shelled
1 tablespoon sherry
1 egg white, slightly beaten
2 tablespoons cornstarch
2 cups vegetable or peanut oil
2 tablespoons chopped
ginger
2 tablespoons chopped
scallion
2 tablespoons chopped garlic
¼ cup rice wine

2 tablespoons hot bean sauce
2 tablespoons hot chili
powder
¼ cup sugar
Dash of sesame oil
Dash of hot oil
Dash of salt
Dash of pepper
¼ cup red vinegar
¾ cup chicken broth
1 tablespoon ketchup

1. Remove black veins from shrimp and rinse. Mix shrimp with sherry, egg white, and 1 tablespoon cornstarch. Heat frying oil to 350°, add shrimp, and stir slowly for 30 seconds. Remove from oil and drain.

2. Add 3 tablespoons of oil to a clean wok and bring to high heat. Add ginger, scallion, and garlic. Stir-fry for 1 minute. Add rice wine, hot bean sauce, hot chili powder, sugar, sesame oil, hot oil, salt, pepper, red vinegar, and chicken broth. Bring to boil. Add shrimp slowly, stirring mixture constantly. Mix 1 tablespoon cornstarch with 3 tablespoons water and add to pan with ketchup. Stir to thicken and serve.

*This spicy dish is complicated to prepare, but well worth the effort. It is essential that every single ingredient be included and that no substitutions be made.*

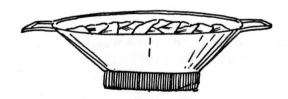

## CRISPY DUCKLING WITH VEGETABLES

*This light and mild Cantonese duck recipe takes a lot of attention and time—four to five hours. Other vegetables in season may be substituted for the ones listed.*

| | |
|---|---|
| 1 (5-pound) Long Island duckling | 3 tablespoons sugar |
| 6 cups plus 3 tablespoons frying oil | 2 eggs, beaten |
| 6 cups chicken broth | ¼ cup flour |
| 3 slices gingerroot | 6 tablespoons cornstarch |
| 2 scallions, green part only, chopped | 1 cup water |
| ¼ teaspoon star anise | 2 teaspoons salt |
| ¼ teaspoon coriander seeds | 1 pound vegetables (mushrooms, water chestnuts, bean sprouts, carrots, snow peas, Chinese cabbage, straw mushrooms, baby corn, bamboo shoots), sliced |
| 12 cinnamon sticks | |
| ¼ teaspoon dried orange peel | |
| ¼ teaspoon fennel | |
| 2 tablespoons light soy sauce | 1 tablespoon oyster sauce |
| 2 tablespoons dark soy sauce | Dash of sesame oil |

1. Clean duck, take the giblets out, and cut the wings off. Heat 6 cups of oil to 350° and lower the duck carefully into the wok with the breast facing down. Fry for 15 minutes. Turn the duck so that the breast is facing up. Fry for 10 minutes. Remove and drain.
2. Bring 4 cups of chicken broth, gingerroot, scallion, anise, coriander seeds, cinnamon sticks, orange peel, fennel, light soy sauce, dark soy sauce, and sugar to boil. Add the duck to the pot, making sure there is enough liquid to cover the whole duck. Add water if more liquid is needed. Boil for 45 minutes over medium heat. Remove and drain duck.
3. When duck cools, cut in half and remove all bones. Place in a dish and press duck down firmly. Put a weight on duck and place in refrigerator for 2 hours to extrude all fat.

4. Combine eggs, flour, 4 tablespoons cornstarch, water, 1 teaspoon salt, and 1 tablespoon oil. Place duck in mixture to cover. Heat cooking oil to 350° again and slowly lower duck into the oil. Cook on each side for about 5 minutes, or until duck turns golden brown. Remove and drain.

5. Add 2 tablespoons of oil to a clean wok and bring it to a high heat. Pour vegetables in and stir-fry for 3 minutes. Add 2 cups chicken broth, oyster sauce, 1 teaspoon salt, a dash of sesame oil, and 2 tablespoons cornstarch. Cook until sauce boils.

6. Chop duck into bite-size pieces and place them on a plate. Pour sauce with vegetables over the duck and serve.

# TANG'S

### FRIED RICE

5 tablespoons peanut or
  vegetable oil
1 egg, beaten
¼ cup small shrimp
¼ cup diced roast pork or ham
¼ cup diced chicken or turkey
¼ cup bean sprouts
6 carrots, sliced

2 mushrooms, sliced
2 water chestnuts, sliced
1 scallion, chopped
4 cups cold, cooked rice
2 tablespoons soy sauce
2 tablespoons chicken broth
½ teaspoon salt

1. Add 3 tablespoons of oil to wok. Bring to high heat, pour egg in, and stir-fry for 1 minute. Add shrimp, pork, chicken, and stir-fry for 1 minute. Add bean sprouts, carrots, mushrooms, water chestnuts, and scallion and stir-fry for another minute. Remove from heat and set aside.
2. Add 2 tablespoons of oil to a clean wok and bring it to medium heat. Carefully break up any lumps in the cooked rice and add to wok. Stir-fry for 5 minutes.
3. Add cooked vegetables, meats, soy sauce, chicken broth, and salt. Stir-fry for 3 more minutes. Serve.

*This light rice dish is a perfect complement to the meal. It is essential to remove all lumps from the rice before cooking.*

# TANG'S

## SEASONAL FRUIT

*For dessert, we serve fresh seasonal fruit cut into finger-size pieces arranged attractively on a platter. As is traditional, we accompany the fruit with hot finger towels for the guests.*

## TEA

*Our tea is half Jasmine and half Oolong. We put the tea leaves directly in the pot and let it steep for 5 minutes. We do not serve sugar, as it destroys the delicate flavor of this refreshing green tea.*

# LaTerrasse

*Dinner for Four*

*Champignons Veroniques*

*Terrine de Canard*

*Nouilles aux Crevettes*

*Sorbet de Pamplemousse*

*Magret de Canard Grillé*

*Salade de Roquette*

*Gâteau Marronier au Chocolat*

*Wines:*

*With the Mushrooms—Delaforce Porto Branco*
*With the Noodles—Giano di Avellino, Mastroberardino, 1978*
*With the Duck—Savigny-Lavières, P. Bitouzet, 1972*
*With the Gâteau—Muscat de Beaunes de Venise, Paul Jaboulet, 1978*

*Judith Wicks and Elliot Cook, Owners*
*Christine Dauber, Chef*

## LA TERRASSE

**La** Terrasse, nestled in what might be called the "left bank" of Philadelphia and housed in three historic rowhouses built in 1870, has a unique flavor of its own. Set amidst the academic and artistic environment of the University of Pennsylvania, Drexel, and the Annenberg Center, it combines the fresh, unpretentious gaiety of a neighborhood bistro with a serious dedication to excellent French cuisine. Judith Wicks says, "We have created the rare combination of a casual atmosphere and serious cuisine. In essence, we hope our guests can relax and have a good time, while enjoying an elegant meal."

The restaurant, started by Elliot Cook fifteen years ago in a fraction of its present space, is now co-owned by Judith Wicks. She describes their partnership: "No one personality dominates La Terrasse. Elliot's sphere is financial and the physical plant; mine is people and atmosphere. Since neither Elliot nor I are gourmet cooks, our chef is free to express her creativity."

As a result of this unusual partnership, the kitchen is a marvel of modern efficiency, the atmosphere is fun and personable, and there are both events and newsletters to create a warm feeling of belonging in all of La Terrasse's clients. The diner may choose to dine in the Piano Room, the scene of nightly concerts on the Steinway grand; the Terrace, built around two huge ailanthus trees; or in one of the more secluded rooms upstairs.

The chef, Christine Dauber, trained at La Varenne École de Cuisine in Paris and formerly worked at Bon Appétit. She is ably aided by Pasquale Iocca, the beverage manager, who "knows as much about wine as anyone in Philadelphia." Christine's cuisine reflects the style of this charming restaurant: an elegant mixture of haute and nouvelle French cuisine.

3432 Sansom Street

### CHAMPIGNONS VERONIQUES

3 ounces cream cheese, at room temperature

1 small garlic clove, finely minced

½ teaspoon minced parsley

½ teaspoon minced chives

½ teaspon minced tarragon

A drop of Tabasco sauce

Salt and white pepper

6 seedless green grapes

12 small mushrooms, stems removed

4 tablespoons butter, melted

3 ounces hard cheese, grated

1. Cream the cream cheese. Add the garlic, herbs, Tabasco, and salt and pepper to taste.
2. Halve the grapes and place one half in each mushroom cap, cut side down. Fill the cap with cheese mixture. Roll the filled cap in butter and then in grated cheese.
3. Place mushrooms on an ungreased baking sheet. Bake in a 400° oven for 15 minutes, or until golden brown. Serve warm, with cocktails or apéritif.

*This unusual recipe blends fruit and cheese to create a piquant taste. It may be prepared in advance and set aside until heated. We serve it with a knife and fork, but toothpicks may be used.*

# LA TERRASSE

## TERRINE DE CANARD AUX POIVRONS VERTS

*This recipe is best made three days in advance so that the flavors can mellow.*

| | |
|---|---|
| 1 (4-pound) duck | ½ teaspoon thyme |
| 4 ounces cognac | 1 tablespoon chopped parsley |
| ½ pound ground veal | 1 egg |
| ½ pound lean pork | 2 or 3 bay leaves |
| ½ pound pork fat | ¼ pound MARINATED |
| Salt and pepper | MUSHROOMS |
| 2 tablespoons green | Cornichons |
| peppercorns (1 tablespoon | Cold vegetables |
| whole, 1 tablespoon | |
| ground) | |

1. To prepare duck and remove the skin intact, turn the duck with its back up. Make an incision down the back and gently pull the skin away down to the breast on each side. Cut the skin off the wing at the first joint and do the same at the leg. Pull the skin inside out at the leg and wing, liberating as much as possible with a small sharp knife. When skin is removed, sprinkle it with a little of the cognac and reserve.
2. Remove all meat from duck, reserving liver. Grind meat with other meats, seasonings, egg, and cognac. Cover with plastic wrap and let rest overnight. Sprinkle duck liver with cognac and reserve as well.
3. The next day, sauté a sample of the meat and correct seasoning. Line a 1½-quart terrine mold, with cover, with the duck skin. Place a layer of half the meat in the bottom. Lay the liver on top. Fill terrine with remaining meat. Place 2 or 3 bay leaves on top and fold the skin over to cover. Seal with 2 layers of aluminum foil. Place in a bain-marie, filled two-thirds of the way to the top of the terrine with boiling water. Bake in 325° oven for about 1½ hours or until a metal skewer inserted in the center for one minute is burning hot when touched to the skin. Pour off accumulated fat, weight with a brick, and refrigerate overnight or for several days.

4. Prepare Marinated Mushrooms.
5. To unmold, dip the mold in hot water and invert. Slice and serve garnished with cornichons, vegetables, and Marinated Mushrooms. Serve with a crock of good mustard and crusty bread.

### MARINATED MUSHROOMS

2 tablespoons lemon juice
4 tablespoons salad oil
    Salt and pepper to taste
1 teaspoon fresh chervil

1 teaspoon fresh parsley
1 teaspoon fresh chives
1 teaspoon shallots, chopped
¼ pound mushrooms

Combine all ingredients except mushrooms. Pour over mushrooms and allow to marinate overnight.

*One clove of garlic may be added to the terrine if desired.*

# LA TERRASSE

## NOUILLES AUX CREVETTES

*This recipe, created by chef Ed Doherty, demands fresh basil. If fresh basil cannot be provided, fresh thyme may be substituted. A hydroponic garden will provide you with all the fresh herbs you need during the year.*

| | | | |
|---|---|---|---|
| 1 | pound fettuccine noodles | 1½ | cups heavy cream |
| | A few drops of olive oil | 28 | jumbo shrimp, dressed and butterflied |
| ½ | pound mushrooms, sliced | | |
| 3 to 4 | shallots, minced | 1 | ounce Pernod |
| 4 | tablespoons unsalted butter | 1 | teaspoon lemon juice |
| | | | Salt and pepper to taste |
| ½ | cup fresh basil, chopped | 1 | cup grated Parmesan cheese |
| | | | Basil leaves, for garnish |

1. Cook noodles al dente in 4 to 5 quarts of salted boiling water for 12 to 15 minutes. Drain, rinse with cold water, and set aside. Toss the pasta with a few drops of olive oil to avoid sticking.
2. Sauté mushrooms and shallots in 3 tablespoons butter for 1 to 2 minutes or until just tender. Add basil and heavy cream and set aside.
3. In a separate pan, heat remaining butter and sauté shrimp for 2 to 3 minutes or until tender. Remove pan from heat, add Pernod, return to heat and flambé until flame subsides completely. Add mushroom mixture and lemon juice and simmer for 5 minutes. Add salt and pepper to taste.
4. Before serving, toss fettuccine with shrimp and mushroom mixture and Parmesan cheese. Serve on warm oval dishes and garnish with basil leaves.

## *LA TERRASSE*

### SORBET DE PAMPLEMOUSSE

*The egg white adds lightness to this delicate dish.*

¾ cup sugar
½ cup water
2 cups grapefruit juice
2 teaspoons grenadine

1 tablespoon grated grapefruit zest
½ egg white, beaten until frothy (optional)
2 stems mint leaves

1. Bring sugar and water to a boil and cook until sugar is dissolved, roughly one minute after boiling. Add ⅓ cup of sugar syrup to grapefruit juice to desired sweetness. Add grenadine and zest and place in ice cream freezer. Stir occasionally until slushy.
2. Add optional egg white if desired and freeze until firm. Allow to season at least 4 hours. Place in refrigerator one hour before serving to soften. Garnish with mint leaves and serve.

# LA TERRASSE

## MAGRET DE CANARD GRILLÉ

4  large (6-ounce) duck
   breasts or 8 (3-ounce)
   breasts
2  shallots, finely minced
1  tablespoon chopped parsley
   Salt and pepper to taste

   Pinch of thyme
   Olive oil to cover,
   approximately 2 cups
2  whole large garlic cloves,
   cut in half

1. Score the fat on the duck breasts by making a grid on top through the fat, not the meat, with the point of a sharp knife. Place in a casserole.
2. Mix shallots and herbs with olive oil and pour over breasts. Marinate in the refrigerator overnight.
3. Heat a charcoal grill and grill the breasts for about 3 minutes on each side, or until they are medium rare. Breasts may also be broiled.
4. Sauté garlic in olive oil until golden brown, 1 to 2 minutes.
5. Slice meat thinly and serve with a grating of black pepper. Serve sautéed garlic on the side.

*Garlic may be puréed and pressed onto the cooked meat. We serve it on the side, for appearance only, since many people, unaware of the difference in taste between cooked and raw garlic, prefer not to eat it. This dish is also well accompanied by brown potatoes and green vegetables.*

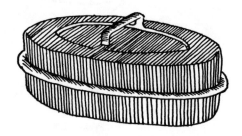

### SALADE DE ROQUETTE

*The pignolias, or pine nuts, add a nutty flavor and enhance the color and texture of this salad.*

| | |
|---|---|
| 1 bunch roquette or arrugula | Salt and pepper |
| 1 head red leaf lettuce | ½ teaspoon tarragon |
| 2 tablespoons red wine vinegar | ⅓ cup olive oil |
| 2 tablespoons Dijon mustard | 2 tablespoons pignolias, toasted |

1. Wash greens, dry and chill well.
2. Combine remaining ingredients except pignolias for a vinaigrette.
3. Assemble greens and pignolias and toss with vinaigrette at serving time.

## GÂTEAU MARRONIER AU CHOCOLAT

*This classic combination of ingredients is a seasonal French specialty, served in the Fall in France when the chestnuts are in season. The recipe serves ten.*

| | |
|---|---|
| 3 ounces semisweet chocolate | 1 tablespoon butter FROSTING |
| 4 eggs, separated | 1 tablespoon flour |
| 1 cup sugar | GLAZE |
| 7 ounces unsweetened chestnut purée (Clement Fougier in cans is recommended) | ½ cup chopped chestnuts or whole candied chestnuts for garnish |

1. Melt chocolate over low heat or in a double boiler. Remove and set aside to cool.
2. Preheat oven to 350°.
3. Beat the egg yolks with ¾ cup of sugar until very light and thickened. Add the chestnut purée and then the cooled chocolate, beating until just mixed.
4. In a separate bowl, beat the egg whites with remaining ¼ cup sugar until stiff but not dry. Fold into the chocolate and chestnut mixture.
5. Pour into a 9" spring-form or layer cake pan which has been buttered and floured. Bake in preheated oven for 30 to 35 minutes. Let the cake cool thoroughly, but do not worry if it falls a bit. It will be dense rather than high.
6. Invert the cake onto a platter and cover with a generous layer of Frosting, making sure it is as smooth as possible. Chill the cake until it is firm to the touch. Pour the glaze over the top and sides of the cake, covering it completely. Garnish with chopped chestnuts or whole candied chestnuts.

### FROSTING

5 ounces semisweet
  chocolate
2 tablespoons water
2 egg yolks

½ cup whipping cream
½ tablespoon rum

1. Melt the chocolate in the water. Beat in the egg yolks over heat until the mixture is thickened. Set aside to cool, but do not allow it to set completely.
2. Whip the cream and fold into cooled chocolate mixture, adding the rum at the last minute.

*If the chocolate is not smooth before adding the whipped cream, add a little liquid cream until it is smoother.*

### GLAZE

4 ounces semisweet
  chocolate

¼ cup rum (preferably dark)
6 ounces softened butter

1. Melt the chocolate with the rum and stir until smooth.
2. Whisk in the butter until completely melted. Let stand until thickened and cool.

*Dinner for Six*

*Homard au Caviar Doré*

*Carré d'Agneau au Coulis d'Echalotes*

*Mousseline de Patates Douces*

*Gratin de Poireau*

*Assiette de Fruits Frais au Caramel*

*Wines:*

*With the Lobster—Pouilly-Fumé, Ladoucette, 1979*

*With the Lamb—Château Latour-Pomerol, 1975*

*With the Fruit—Château La Tour-Blanche, Sauternes, 1975*

*Leslie Smith and Jeannine Mermet, Proprietors*

*Jean-François Taquet, Chef*

# LA TRUFFE

**To** enter La Truffe is to enter a world of charm and elegance, reinforced by the warm "bon soir" with which Jeannine Mermet and her husband Les Smith greet their guests. Exquisitely arranged flowers on lavishly appointed tables, wood beams borrowed from an old French inn, and luxurious patterned pillows create a delightful aura of sumptuous Gallic intimacy. Les says, "The restaurant is a reflection of our personal taste," and Jeannine adds, "We are small enough so that the two of us and our chef Jean-François can personally supervise everything down to the smallest details, whether it is tasting a sauce in the kitchen, making selections from our extensive wine cellar, or personally greeting our guests."

Recently, La Truffe began serving nouvelle cuisine. Says Les, "After sixteen years, we decided it was time for a change. Nouvelle cuisine is more appropriate to the way people live today. Everyone wants to eat lightly. With nouvelle cuisine, a five-course meal is possible and not overwhelming. Jeannine and I found a brilliant and innovative young chef and we are delighted with the results. So are our many regular clients, who have greeted the change with enthusiasm."

The chef, Jean-François Taquet, trained at Restaurant Girardet in Lausanne, Switzerland, and has been in Philadelphia only a short while. When asked to explain his philosophy of cooking, he said, "My recipes are all original. Nouvelle cuisine allows me to be creative. The essential principle of nouvelle cuisine is to bring out the natural flavors of the food by using no flour or butter. That's why I demand completely fresh ingredients and I even import special items from France, such as foie gras, twenty-five-year-old vinegar, and the purest of cooking oils. I do everything I can to insure that all my ingredients are of the first quality."

The menu is entirely in French because, as Les says, "We prefer that our well-versed waiters explain the dishes. We hope that our clients will feel that they have stepped into another environment when they come here." It is not surprising that La Truffe is a recurrent choice for those Philadelphians who prefer to dine in just such a gracious and inviting special environment.

10 South Front Street

## HOMARD AU CAVIAR DORÉ

6 (1-pound) lobsters
1 teaspoon olive oil
1 leek, chopped
1 large carrot, chopped
1 head garlic, peeled and
   chopped
1 large white onion, chopped

2 shallots, chopped
1 bay leaf
A sprig of fresh thyme, or
1 teaspoon dried thyme
2 cups heavy cream
4 ounces golden caviar
Salt and pepper

1. Cook lobsters in boiling water for 3 minutes. Remove and split in half, cutting across the back. Crack claws. Remove meat, keeping the pieces whole. Remove coral and reserve in the refrigerator.
2. Sauté lobster shells in a hot pan with olive oil for 3 or 4 minutes to flavor the pan. Add washed and chopped vegetables to the pan and sauté lightly for 3 to 4 minutes, or until slightly browned. Add herbs and cream. Bring to a boil for 5 minutes to reduce. Turn off heat and allow mixture to steep for 10 minutes.
3. Pass mixture through a sieve. The sauce that emerges will be quite thick.
4. Reheat sauce in pot over a low flame, stirring constantly. Reduce until the sauce coats the back of a spoon. Add lobster meat and reheat for 2 minutes, or just enough to warm the lobster. Add golden caviar to the sauce and season with salt and pepper.
5. Arrange meat on a hot plate. Spoon the sauce around the lobster and serve.

*The lobster roe may be added to this dish at the chef's discretion. If the roe is added when sauce is reheated, the sauce will turn pink, eliminating the contrast between the golden caviar sauce and the pinkish lobster.*

### CARRÉ D'AGNEAU AU COULIS D'ECHALOTES

*This lamb dish is typical of the nouvelle cuisine. It is simple, light, and pure with a minimum of cooking time.*

3 racks of lamb, shin bones removed and trimmed of fat, cut into 24 chops
1 teaspoon olive oil
1 cup consommé (for home use, prepared consommé may be used)

1½ cups BROWN SAUCE
5 shallots, finely chopped
Salt and pepper

1. Sauté the chops in a heavy-bottomed skillet at a high temperature in olive oil. Cook each side 2 minutes so that lamb is golden brown on the outside and pink inside. If the temperature of the pot is correct, the chop will sizzle when it is put in. Remove chops and put on the side.
2. Pour excess fat out of the sauté pan, leaving the scrapings. Add consommé and reduce for 5 minutes at high heat. Add Brown Sauce and reduce for 2 minutes. Add shallots and cook for another 5 minutes. Season to taste with salt and pepper.
3. Strain sauce through a fine sieve. Put in a blender at high speed for about 30 seconds.
4. Heat chops in a 350° oven for 5 minutes. Arrange chops in a crisscross pattern, 4 to a plate with bones crossing. Pour sauce around meat. Serve.

*The blender makes the sauce lighter and will correct the consistency if the sauce is not reduced enough.*

### BROWN SAUCE

10 pounds veal bones or
   knuckles
1 onion
1 carrot
2 stalks celery

2 bay leaves
½ teaspoon thyme
3 tablespoons tomato paste,
   or 2 whole tomatoes

1. Bake bones in a 350° oven for about 45 minutes to remove fat and to brown.
2. Put bones in a large heavy stock pot and add enough water to cover the bones by 3″. Roughly chop vegetables and add them to the pot with herbs and tomato paste.
3. Simmer uncovered for at least 6 hours, or until the sauce is reduced by half. Occasionally skim the top of the pot to remove residue.
4. Strain liquid, discarding pulp and bones. Reduce liquid by half again over high heat until it coats the spoon.

### MOUSSELINE DE PATATES DOUCE

5 young sweet potatoes,
  approximately 1½ pounds
1 tablespoon sweet butter
2 tablespoons heavy cream

Dash of salt
Dash of pepper
Dash of nutmeg

Boil whole potatoes in salted water until they are cooked through, about 20 minutes. Cut them up and put in blender with butter, heavy cream, and seasonings. Blend together until the consistency is the same as mashed potatoes.

*We pipe the potatoes onto the plate. When served with the lamb, we make several mounds around the lamb and spoon the sauce in between to create a colorful and decorative effect.*

### GRATIN DE POIREAU

2 leeks
  Salt and pepper

½ cup whipped cream
6 ounces Swiss cheese, grated

1. Cut and clean leeks. Boil for 2 minutes in water to cover and immediately put under cold water to preserve color and taste.
2. Put leeks in 6 small ramekins or one large ovenproof casserole. Add salt and pepper and put whipped cream over them. Add grated Swiss cheese on the top. Brown under broiler for 1 minute and put in oven at 350° for a few minutes to heat all the way through. Serve.

*This dish can be prepared ahead of time, refrigerated, and heated just before serving.*

### ASSIETTE DE FRUITS FRAIS AU CARAMEL

| | |
|---|---|
| 7 tablespoons sugar | 5½ tablespoons whipped cream |
| 1 teaspoon water | Fresh fruit of the season |

1. Cook sugar and water in pan until sugar caramelizes, for about 2 to 3 minutes or until it turns brown. Refrigerate. When sugar is cold, add whipped cream, beating by hand.
2. Prepare fresh fruit by cleaning and cutting into finger-size pieces. Arrange decoratively around plate with an eye to color and symmetry.
3. Put the caramel mixture on top of fruit. Put under a broiler and watch it carefully until it browns, about 30 to 40 seconds.

*This delicate dessert is an enticing blend of textures and tastes. The hot caramel complements the cold fruits and the result is deliciously light.*

*Dinner for Four*

Crab Normande

Potage Crécy

Poulet Rôti à la Moutarde

Choux Fleur Mornay

Haricots Verts à la Lyonnaise

Salade de Poireaux, Tiede, Sauce Vinaigrette

Soufflé Glacé Grand Marnier

Wines:

With the Crab—Chappelet Vineyard Chenin Blanc, 1978

With the Chicken—Clos du Val Zinfandel Nouvelle

Vincent J. Alberici, Executive Chef

David L. Kacala, Versailles Chef

# VERSAILLES

The Versailles at the Bellevue Stratford is described by Executive Chef Vincent J. Alberici as "a dining experience, rather than simply an eating experience." He continues, "The room is designed for total comfort, as a backdrop for the excellent food we serve. The extra things are what count—the quality of the service, the fresh flowers at every table, the homemade bon bons, and first and foremost, of course, the cuisine itself."

The decor utilizes soft high-backed chairs, muted colors, subdued lighting, and warm, velvety walls to create a feeling of intimacy for each diner. The three separate dining alcoves, insuring a complete feeling of privacy, are thrown into relief by the copper and brass ceiling and the cascading chandeliers from Uruguay. Soft classical music provides an undertone, while the ambitious display of wines encourages careful selection.

Chef Alberici says, "We go to enormous pains to make this a unique dining experience. At lunch, we typically serve country French cuisine; at dinner, traditional French.

"We also delight in planning special holiday dinners. The Versailles has its own chef and kitchen, so that all of our dishes may be prepared to order. On a daily basis, we offer twelve to fifteen classical sauces, all naturally reduced without the addition of flour."

The pastry chef, Gunther Heiland, is a Master Chef, a rare title. In 1980, he won a gold medal at the International Culinary Olympics in Germany. Chef Alberici says, "He creates magnificent sculptures with edible products. Chocolate is his specialty."

For elegant, comfortable dining and an opportunity to feel pleasantly pampered, the Versailles is an obvious choice.

Bellevue Stratford
Broad at Walnut Street

### CRAB NORMANDE

*"Normandy" denotes the use of apples and apple brandy. This dish blends two textures, the softness of the crabmeat and the crunchiness of the apples.*

12  ounces fresh lump
    crabmeat
1  cup mayonnaise
4  ounces Calvados
1½ to 2  apples, diced

1  small head leaf lettuce
4  mint leaves
1  tablespoon chopped fresh
    chives

1.  Combine crabmeat with mayonnaise, Calvados, and diced apple.
2.  Place in bed of lettuce leaves and garnish with chives and mint.

### POTAGE CRÉCY

*This simple but classical soup is rarely served yet is easily within the reach of the average cook.*

1  tablespoon butter
1  small onion, roughly
    chopped
1½  carrots, finely grated
1  slice fresh ginger

2  cups chicken stock
¼  cup water
1  cup heavy cream
    Salt and pepper
    Chopped parsley or chives

1.  Melt butter in 2½ quart saucepan. Add onion and cook for 2 minutes. Add carrots, cover, reduce heat, and steam for 5 minutes.
2.  Add ginger, chicken stock and water. Cook 25 minutes.
3.  Purée in food processor or blender. Return to pot and bring to boil. Add heavy cream and bring again to boil. Season with salt and pepper.
4.  Garnish each serving with chopped parsley or chives.

### POULET RÔTI, A LA MOUTARD

*This simple, inexpensive dish is both interesting and elegant.*

2 (3-pound) frying chickens
  Salt and pepper to taste
½ cup Dijon mustard

½ cup fresh bread crumbs
  seasoned with:
  Pinch of thyme
  Pinch of sage
  Pinch of parsley
  Pinch of rosemary

1. Preheat oven to 500°.
2. Have your butcher remove the backbone of the chickens. Flatten the chicken by cracking the breastbone. Remove excess fat and sprinkle with salt and pepper.
3. Place chicken in a shallow baking pan. Cook in preheated oven for 25 minutes.
4. Remove from oven and apply mustard with a pastry brush. Sprinkle the bread crumbs over the mustard. Use the fat in the baking pan to coat the bread crumbs. Return to the oven and cook for 5 to 10 minutes more.
5. Remove from oven, quarter each chicken, and serve.

### CHOUX FLEUR MORNAY

1 head cauliflower
  Juice of 1 lemon
1 cup MORNAY SAUCE

2 tablespoons grated
  Parmesan cheese

1. Blanch the whole head of cauliflower in boiling salted water to cover to which the juice of the lemon has been added. Cook 8 to 10 minutes, or until just tender. Remove and run under cold water.
2. Break cauliflower into florets. Place in a gratin dish. Cover with Mornay Sauce. Sprinkle with grated cheese.
3. Place in 350° oven for 10 minutes.

# VERSAILLES

### MORNAY SAUCE

4 tablespoons butter
4 tablespoons flour
1 cup milk

2 ounces grated Swiss cheese
3 tablespoons heavy cream
Salt and pepper to taste

1. Melt butter in a small heavy pan. Add the flour and mix well.
2. Slowly add milk and bring to boil. Allow to cook for 5 minutes over low heat.
3. Add cheese and heavy cream. Remove from heat, whisk, and season to taste.

*If desired, other varieties of cheese may be substituted for the Swiss cheese.*

## HARICOTS VERTS A LA LYONNAISE

*This is a typical French country dish. The most important thing to remember is not to overcook the vegetables, causing loss of color, nutrients, and crispness.*

1 pound fresh green beans,
  cut into uniform strips
2 tablespoons butter

1 tablespoon vegetable oil
3 tablespoons chopped
  shallots

1. Blanch string beans in boiling salted water to cover for 2 minutes. Drain and cool with water.
2. Melt butter and oil. When foaming, add shallots. Cook for 3 minutes. Add green beans and warm just long enough to bring to serving temperature.

## SALADE DE POIREAUX, TIEDE, SAUCE VINAIGRETTE

2   *bunches fresh leeks*
    *Salt*
2   *tablespoons white wine*
    *vinegar*

2   *tablespoons virgin press*
    *olive oil*
    *Cracked black pepper*

1.  To trim the leeks, leave about 2" of green attached as well as a small piece of root end. Starting at the green end, cut down length of leek about three-fourths of the way down. Turn leek one-quarter and slit through. Clean thoroughly under running water.
2.  Place leeks in pan, barely covered with water. Add salt and vinegar. Cook for 3 minutes, or until tender.
3.  Remove and discard root end. Slice in half lengthwise and allow to drain.
4.  Cover with oil, drop by drop, while leek is still warm. Season with cracked black pepper and serve.

*The key to this unusual and simple salad is the use of virgin press olive oil, which adds an extraordinary taste. The oil may be purchased at most food specialty shops.*

### SOUFFLÉ GLACÉ GRAND MARNIER

6 *eggs*
½ *cup sugar*
1 *pint heavy cream, whipped*

3 *ounces Grand Marnier*
*A few drops of vanilla*

1. Prepare a 1-quart soufflé dish by wrapping aluminum foil around the inside. Allow foil to extend 3" above the rim of the dish.
2. Beat eggs and sugar in a mixing bowl over a simmering double boiler. When mixture is warm, remove and hand whip at high speed until eggs are fluffy and mixture forms soft peaks.
3. Fold in whipped cream, Grand Marnier, and vanilla. Pour mixture into mold and freeze for at least 4 hours.
4. Remove foil collar and serve.

*This classical French dessert is not too delicate to prepare because it is cold.*

# VICTOR Cafe

*Dinner for Four*

*Roasted Peppers with Garlic and Olive Oil*

*Stracciatella*

*Saltimbocca Barone Scarpia*

*Pasta al'Olio*

*Tomato Stuffed with Spinach and Herbs*

*Victor Salad*

*Zabaglione*

*Wine:*

*Montepulciano di Abruzzo, Duchi di Castelluccio, VQPRD*

*Henry and Lola Di Stefano, Owners*

*Jeffrey Gutstein, Chef*

The Victor Cafe, a Philadelphia landmark, has appealed to music lovers and aficionados of good Italian food for nearly fifty years. As Gregory Di Stefano, grandson of the original owner, says, "It is probably the oldest family establishment in Philadelphia. My sister Pamela and I try to extend the family feeling we have about the Victor Cafe to all of our guests."

Originally a record shop, the Victor Cafe, named after the famous Victor Talking Machine Company, became a restaurant in 1933. Its proprietor, John Di Stefano, maintained his love of opera and opened a small, cosy restaurant that was "as close as he could come to presenting nightly concerts without actually owning an opera hall." Gregory points at the records and signed photographs that line the walls. "We have one of the most extensive record collections in the country, including some very rare recordings. If our guests are not dining to Caruso, Chaliapin, or Pavarotti, they may be entertained by one of our waiters, many of whom are aspiring singers and who tend to burst into song spontaneously. One such aspiring singer—Mario Lanza—used to beg for extra food with the promise, 'Someday you'll pay to hear me sing!' "

Chef Jeffrey Gutstein, who trained at the Culinary Institute of America, describes his cuisine as "primarily Southern Italian, with some Northern touches." He adds, "I am a very creative chef, but I base all my recipes upon the traditional Italian dishes. Soon, we hope to create a new menu with many dishes named for the opera stars who frequent the Victor Cafe."

From the original Nipper dog which stands guard over the bar to the warmth and romantic charm that are the hallmarks of the Victor Cafe, Gregory is determined to "maintain the flavor" of the restaurant. He says proudly, "Customers that haven't been here in forty years say it looks exactly the same. To achieve this kind of continuity is not easy, but Pamela and I intend to devote ourselves to it. After all, how many families have their own opera gallery?"

The Victor Cafe is a must for all who enjoy Italian food, or opera, or a mélange of the two. Both are served *con gusto* in a delightfully appealing setting.

1303 Dickinson Street

## ROASTED PEPPERS WITH GARLIC AND OLIVE OIL

6 *Italian green peppers, washed*
⅓ *cup olive oil*
*Salt and white pepper*

4 *romaine leaves*
6 *cloves garlic, finely minced*
1½ *tablespoons chopped parsley*

1. Preheat oven to 375°. Put whole peppers on sheet pan and lightly coat with olive oil. Season with salt and pepper. Roast for 7 to 8 minutes or until golden brown. Remove peppers and allow to cool.
2. Cut peppers in half, core and de-seed. Slice peppers lengthwise in ½" strips.
3. In small oval dishes, place one leaf of romaine and place pepper strips widthwise along plate. Sprinkle garlic on peppers, drip remaining oil over, and garnish with parsley.

*Keep garlic in 1 tablespoon olive oil and it will not turn brown.*

## STRACCIATELLA

1 *quart CHICKEN STOCK (see next page)*
6 *ounces Parmesan cheese, grated*

2 *eggs*
½ *pound spinach, cleaned and cut in julienne strips*
*Salt and pepper*

1. Put Chicken Stock in a kettle and bring to boil over high heat. Add 5 ounces of cheese and stir.
2. Break eggs in bowl and slightly whip, just to break up yolks. Add eggs to stock slowly, whipping continually, so that boiling continues. Drop spinach in and return to boil. Season to taste.
3. Garnish soup with remaining cheese and serve.

*It is essential to use care in folding eggs into stock as the stock must continue to boil.*

## CHICKEN STOCK

3 pounds chicken necks and
backbones
1 pound onions, roughly cut
½ pound carrots, roughly cut
½ pound celery, roughly cut

3 stems parsley
1 small bay leaf
Pinch of thyme
Salt and white pepper

Combine all ingredients in stock pot, covering with water by 1½". Bring to boil and reduce to simmer. Skim periodically and simmer uncovered for 2½ to 3 hours. Pass through a fine strainer.

## SALTIMBOCCA BARONE SCARPIA

4 tablespoons clarified butter
1 pound veal, cut into 16
(1-ounce) medallions,
pounded paper thin
½ cup flour to dredge veal
Small pinch of sage
3 ounces Marsala wine
2 ounces prosciutto, sliced
paper thin

2 ounces mozzarella, very
thinly sliced
5 ounces mushrooms,
thinly sliced
1 cup BROWN SAUCE
Salt and white pepper
1½ tablespoons chopped
parsley

1. Place sauté pan over high heat and add 2 tablespoons of clarified butter. Dredge medallions in flour and add to pan when the butter reaches the smoking point. Sauté for 30 seconds on each side. Add sage and wine and remove from heat.
2. Keeping veal in pan, shingle the medallions over each other to create 4 separate portions. Place prosciutto and mozzarella slices over each portion to cover.
3. Place in a 350° oven for 3 minutes or until cheese melts. Remove.
4. Sauté mushrooms in 2 tablespoons clarified butter for 3 minutes. Add mushrooms to veal, return to heat and add Brown Sauce, swirling pan to heat. Adjust seasonings.
5. Remove with spatula to serving plates and ladle sauce over veal. Garnish with parsley.

# VICTOR CAFE

## BROWN SAUCE

6 tablespoons butter
8 tablespoons flour
1 quart College Inn
beef stock

1 bay leaf
Pinch of thyme
6 tablespoons tomato purée
Salt and white pepper

1. Melt butter in pan and stir in flour. Cook 8 to 10 minutes, constantly stirring until brown.
2. In another pan, warm broth and add half of the browned butter, or roux, whisking constantly. Add second half, still whisking. Add bay leaf, thyme, and tomato purée. Add salt and pepper to taste. Bring mixture to boil and reduce to simmer, skimming occasionally. Cook for 2½ to 3 hours until the mixture coats the back of the spoon.
3. Strain through a fine sieve.

*My beef stock takes over 12 to 15 hours to cook and demi-glace takes an additional 4 hours, so here is my quick home brown sauce.*


## PASTA AL'OLIO

½ pound thin spaghetti
4 ounces olive oil
4 cloves garlic, finely minced

Salt and white pepper
2 tablespoons chopped
parsley

1. Cook spaghetti in 1 quart of boiling salted water for 6 to 8 minutes or until al dente. Drain immediately.
2. Place oil in sauté pan and heat over medium flame. Add garlic and sauté until soft but not burned.
3. Add pasta, salt, and white pepper to taste. Add parsley, swirling the pan until pasta is hot. Serve.

*This light pasta dish is a perfect accompaniment to any entrée.*

## TOMATO STUFFED WITH SPINACH

*Be sure not to overcook this dish as the tomatoes will become mushy.*

| | |
|---|---|
| 4 medium-size tomatoes | Pinch of basil |
| 1½ pounds spinach, cleaned, stems removed | Pinch of oregano |
| | Salt and white pepper |
| 3 ounces minced onions | 3 ounces bread crumbs |
| 2 tablespoons clarified butter | |
| 3 ounces Parmesan cheese, grated | |

1. Core the tomatoes. Turn them over and with a knife, cut into each one around the sides all the way down so that a cone shape emerges.
2. Cook spinach in 3 tablespoons of water for 3 minutes, stirring frequently. Remove spinach and drain in colander, squeezing out all moisture. Chop spinach finely.
3. Sauté onion in 1 tablespoon of clarified butter until translucent. Add spinach and sauté for 2 minutes. Add Parmesan cheese, basil, oregano, salt and white pepper to taste, and bread crumbs. Allow mixture to tighten by cooking for 2 minutes, stirring constantly. Remove and cool.
4. Stuff the tomatoes with spinach mixture. Place on a sheet pan and sprinkle with remaining clarified butter. Cook at 350° for 8 to 10 minutes, or until the tomatoes are soft. Remove and serve.

## VICTOR SALAD

| | |
|---|---|
| 1 head iceberg lettuce | 2 medium tomatoes, cut into eighths |
| 2 eggs, hard-cooked and roughly chopped | VICTOR SALAD DRESSING |

Core and clean lettuce. Tear with hands. Toss with eggs and tomato. Pour dressing on salad.

### *VICTOR SALAD DRESSING*

6 *ounces vegetable oil*
2 *ounces white vinegar*
1 *tablespoon sugar*
2 *tablespoons lemon juice*
2 *cloves garlic, minced*

*Pinch of basil*
*Pinch of oregano*
*Salt and white pepper*
4 *ounces Gorgonzola cheese, broken*

Mix all ingredients together.

*This unusual dressing is an old family recipe.*

## ZABAGLIONE

8 *egg yolks*
3 *tablespoons water*
  *Marsala wine*
  *Grand Marnier*
½ *cup confectioners' sugar*

¼ *teaspoon vanilla*
1 *pint heavy cream*
1 *ounce semisweet chocolate, shaved with a knife*

1. Place eggs, water, wine, and Grand Marnier in the top of a double boiler. Add half the sugar and whip at a medium boil until it is a thick lemony color and the mixture forms a ribbon when whisk is lifted. Remove and let cool.
2. Whip remaining sugar, vanilla, and heavy cream until the mixture forms stiff peaks. Fold the lemony mixture into whipped cream with a rubber spatula.
3. Pour into parfait glasses and garnish with chocolate shavings. Chill and serve.

*If you don't whip the eggs quickly, you may end up with scrambled eggs.*

# Wildflowers

*Dinner for Four*

*Caribbean Fruit Soup*

*Green Bean, Mushroom, and Tomato Salad*

*Bay Scallops Vin Blanc*

*Veal Oscar Wildflowers*

*Tarte "Coeur à la Crème"*

*Wines:*

*With the Scallops—Round Hill Chardonnay, 1979*

*With the Veal—Brunello di Montalcino, Villa Banfi, 1971*

*With the Tarte—Château Voigny, Sauternes, 1969*

*Ken Barnett, Chef Patron de Cuisine*

*Peter Howell, Chef*

# WILDFLOWERS

The creation of Wildflowers ten years ago was "a labour of love" for its owner, sculptor Ken Barnett. "It allowed me," he says, "to express myself as an artist through the medium of the business world. I consider Wildflowers a complete expression of a very special point of view about life, both in cuisine and decor."

Chef Peter Howell describes his menu as a mixture of European cuisine, from haute to country French to American. He speaks of food discriminatingly and lovingly. "To me, the process of food preparation is an art in itself. I most enjoy, as my repertoire grows, to integrate traditional French recipes with other, newer touches, so that our menu is always original." The use of an extensive and changeable *carte du jour* allows Peter ample scope for the creation of new dishes.

Wildflowers' dramatic salad bar is justly famous for its lavishly displayed fresh vegetables, bearing out Ken Barnett's contention that "my clients must be able to eat with their eyes, too." His wine list is extensive and his *vins du jour* are always interesting. Yet he insists that the cuisine he serves must always be "accessible to my clients and never, never pretentious."

After opening, Wildflowers became a mecca for artists. Its warmly inviting atmosphere, enhanced by the magnificent use of stained glass, hand-painted tiles, frescoed walls, and many antiques, creates a perfect frame for the ever-changing exhibitions of local artists on its walls, often heralded by an opening party. A relaxed and comfortable way to dine elegantly, Wildflowers justly fulfills Ken Barnett's favorite quotation from Escoffier: "Good cooking is the basis of true happiness."

516 South Fifth Street

## CARIBBEAN FRUIT SOUP

*This delicious cold soup can be prepared a day in advance. Depending upon the seasonal fruits that are available, the ingredients can be changed to suit your fancy. Simply adjust the amount of sweetness to taste.*

| | |
|---|---|
| 1  cup sugar | 1  orange, roughly chopped |
| 1  cup water | 1  lemon, roughly chopped |
| ½  cup white wine | 2  tablespoons arrowroot |
| 1  cinnamon stick | 1  cup diced fruit |
| 5  cloves | CINNAMON TOAST |
| 4  cups roughly chopped mixed fruit (strawberries should definitely be included. We use melons, papaya, mangos, cherries, grapes, etc.) | |

1. In a large pot over medium-high heat, mix sugar into water until dissolved. Add wine, spices, and fruit. Simmer 30 minutes. Mix arrowroot with a little water and add to soup at a rapid boil. Return to boil and simmer for 5 minutes or until soup coats the back of a spoon. Cool.
2. Pour through a sieve, pressing fruit to extract all the liquid.
3. Serve in glass bowls and garnish with fresh fruit. Serve with Cinnamon Toast triangles on the side.

*We serve this soup over a bowl of crushed ice.*


### *CINNAMON TOAST*

| | |
|---|---|
| 8  slices bread | 2  teaspoons cinnamon |
| 2  tablespoons butter | |

Toast bread. Cut into triangle shapes. Spread with butter and sprinkle with cinnamon.

# WILDFLOWERS

## GREEN BEAN, MUSHROOM, AND TOMATO SALAD

*At Wildflowers, where we are known for our salad buffet, we try to keep our ingredients in the most natural form possible.*

| | |
|---|---|
| ¾  pound green beans | VINAIGRETTE |
| ¾  pound mushrooms | 2  heads Bibb lettuce, |
| ½  pound tomatoes | washed, leaves separated |

1. Clean and blanch green beans in boiling salted water to cover for 5 minutes. Clean mushrooms, remove stems, and slice. Skin, seed, and dice tomatoes.
2. Combine ingredients with Vinaigrette and serve in Bibb lettuce cups.

### VINAIGRETTE

| | |
|---|---|
| 2  teaspoons Dijon mustard | Salt and freshly ground |
| ⅓  cup tarragon vinegar | pepper |
| 1  cup light vegetable oil | |
| 2  tablespoons finely minced fresh tarragon leaves | |

In a stainless steel bowl, combine mustard with vinegar. Add oil while whisking with a steel whip. Finish by adding tarragon and salt and pepper.

*The Vinaigrette may be made ahead of time and refrigerated. It is essential to use fresh tarragon. The taste is just not the same with dried tarragon.*

### BAY SCALLOPS VIN BLANC

*This dish has an unusual combination of flavors—the dry wine as a contrast to the sweet scallops, the leek to add a certain strength, and the nice blend of the cream base. It is light enough to be an appetizer although it may be served as an entrée. We serve it with puff pastry in fish-shaped fleurons.*

| | |
|---|---|
| 1 large leek, julienned | ¾ cup dry vermouth |
| 2 tablespoons butter | 1½ cups heavy cream |
| 1¼ pounds fresh bay scallops | Salt and pepper |

1. Sauté the leek in butter over low heat for 4 to 5 minutes or until tender, but not brown. Add scallops and vermouth and simmer for approximately 5 minutes. Remove scallops and keep warm.
2. Reduce vermouth by half over medium-high flame for 4 to 5 minutes. Add cream and reduce over medium heat until thick, stirring.
3. Add salt and pepper to taste and pour sauce over scallops and serve.

## VEAL OSCAR WILDFLOWERS

*This dish, combining meat, seafood, and a vegetable, is our house specialty. The unique treatment of two classic French ingredients—the béarnaise sauce and the demi-glace—illustrates Wildflower's culinary forté—a blend of the old and the new.*

| | |
|---|---|
| 16 medium-size spears asparagus | 8 ounces King crabmeat, preferably fresh |
| 4 (4-ounce) veal medallions Flour for dusting | *BÉARNAISE SAUCE* |
| 2 eggs, beaten | *DEMI-GLACE* |
| ¼ cup clarified butter | |

1. Trim and peel asparagus. Steam for 3 minutes or cook in boiling water to cover for 3 to 4 minutes. Keep warm.
2. Pound veal until thin. Dust with flour and dip into beaten eggs. Sauté in butter at medium-high heat for approximately 2 minutes on each side, or until brown. For the last 2 minutes, add crabmeat in large pieces to heat.
3. To serve, place crab over veal and top with Béarnaise Sauce. Surround with 4 asparagus spears topped with Demi-Glace.

### *BÉARNAISE SAUCE*

| | |
|---|---|
| 1 tablespoon finely minced fresh tarragon | 3 egg yolks |
| ½ tablespoon minced shallots | 2 teaspoons cold water |
| ½ teaspoon cracked black pepper | 1 cup butter, melted, at room temperature |
| ½ cup vinegar | ½ lemon, juiced |
| | ½ teaspoon salt |

1. Combine tarragon, shallots, pepper, and vinegar in a small pot and cook over high heat until vinegar is completely evaporated. Set aside.
2. Using a stainless steel bowl over a pot of simmering water, cook the egg yolks and water, beating constantly with a wire whisk until slightly stiff and creamy, about 5 minutes.
3. Take off the heat and slowly add butter while continuing the beating motion, thus creating a smooth sauce.
4. Add lemon juice and salt. Add tarragon reduction to finish sauce.

### DEMI-GLACE

| | |
|---|---|
| 6 pounds veal, beef, or chicken bones | 6 peppercorns |
| 1 carrot, diced | 2 bay leaves |
| 1 onion, diced | ¼ teaspoon thyme |
| 1 tablespoon tomato paste, or 3 tomatoes, diced | 8 quarts water |
| | 2 tablespoons butter |
| | 2 tablespoons flour |
| ½ teaspoon salt | ½ cup Madeira |

1. Roast bones in a 425° oven for approximately 20 minutes or until brown. Transfer to a large stock pot and add carrot, onion, tomato paste, salt, peppercorns, bay leaves, thyme, and water. Simmer for at least 2 hours. Strain.
2. Prepare a roux by melting butter and adding flour with a whisk. Cook for 5 minutes over medium heat, stirring occasionally. Add roux to strained stock and return to heat. Cook approximately 1 hour, or until mixture is reduced to about 1 quart. Add Madeira.

## TARTE "COEUR A LA CRÈME"

1 *cup flour*
1 *cup ground toasted*
  *almonds*
½ *teaspoon baking powder*
  *Zest of 1 lemon*
5 *tablespoons butter*
2 *tablespoons shortening*
2 *egg yolks*

1 *teaspoon vanilla*
  *CREAM CHEESE FILLING*
1 *quart fresh strawberries,*
  *hulled*
⅓ *cup apricot jam*
⅓ *cup water, brandy, apricot*
  *flavored liqueur, or*
  *light rum*

1. Preheat oven to 350°.
2. Combine flour, almonds, baking powder and lemon zest. Cut butter and shortening into small pieces and work into dry ingredients with a pastry cutter, fork, or hand. Add egg yolks and vanilla. Continue to mix until dough is smooth.
3. Press dough into a 9″ or 10″ tart pan with a removable bottom, forming sides that are ¼″ to ½″ high. Line the shell with parchment or cheesecloth and fill with rice. Bake in preheated oven for 15 to 20 minutes. Remove rice and brown the shell for no more than 5 minutes. Cool.
4. Fill the pastry shell with Cream Cheese Filling. Chill to set for at least 15 minutes. Top with strawberries, either whole or halved, arranged in concentric circles.
5. Prepare apricot glaze by simmering apricot jam with water, brandy, liqueur, or rum. Within 10 minutes, the jam should be thoroughly melted and the mixture should be smooth. Allow to cool slightly. Glaze the strawberries and the edge of the crust with the warm apricot glaze.
6. When ready to serve, remove tart from pan and transfer to a plate.

*This tart is best if it is served the day it is made. You may coat the bottom of the baked pastry shell with 4 to 6 ounces of melted semisweet chocolate or the apricot glaze. If so, be sure to allow this layer to chill before adding the cream cheese.*

# WILDFLOWERS

## CREAM CHEESE FILLING

8 ounces cream cheese,
  softened
1 cup sour cream
¼ cup confectioners' sugar

3 tablespoons vanilla
1 tablespoon unflavored
  gelatin
¼ cup water

1. While tart shell is cooking, combine cream cheese, sour cream, sugar, and vanilla; mix until smooth.
2. In a saucepan, sprinkle gelatin over water and place pan over medium heat. Stir until gelatin is thoroughly dissolved. Combine with cream cheese mixture.

# RECIPE INDEX

## Appetizers

## Beverages

## Desserts and Dessert Accents

# RECIPE INDEX

## Entrées

## Pastas

## Salads

## Salad Dressings

# RECIPE INDEX

## Sauces, Stocks, and Special Seasonings

# DINING IN–THE GREAT CITIES
## *A Collection of Gourmet Recipes from the Finest Chefs in the Country*

Each book contains gourmet recipes for complete meals from the chefs of 21 great restaurants.

| | | | |
|---|---|---|---|
| ___ *Dining In–Baltimore* | $7.95 | ___ *Dining In–Pittsburgh* | *7.95* |
| ___ *Dining In–Boston* | *7.95* | ___ *Dining In–Portland* | *7.95* |
| ___ *Dining In–Chicago, Vol. II* | *8.95* | ___ *Dining In–St. Louis* | *7.95* |
| ___ *Dining In–Dallas* | *7.95* | ___ *Dining In–San Francisco* | *7.95* |
| ___ *Dining In–Denver* | *7.95* | ___ *Dining In–Seattle, Vol. II* | *7.95* |
| ___ *Dining In–Hawaii* | *7.95* | ___ *Dining In–Sun Valley* | *7.95* |
| ___ *Dining In–Houston, Vol. I* | *7.95* | ___ *Dining In–Toronto* | *7.95* |
| ___ *Dining In–Houston, Vol. II* | *7.95* | ___ *Dining In–Vancouver, B.C.* | *8.95* |
| ___ *Dining In–Kansas City* | *7.95* | ___ *Feasting In Atlanta* | *7.95* |
| ___ *Dining In–Los Angeles* | *7.95* | ___ *Feasting In New Orleans* | *7.95* |
| ___ *Dining In–Milwaukee* | *7.95* | **Forthcoming Titles —** | |
| ___ *Dining In–Minneapolis/St. Paul* | *7.95* | ___ *Dining In–Cleveland* | *8.95* |
| ___ *Dining In–Monterey Peninsula* | *7.95* | ___ *Dining In–Manhattan* | *8.95* |
| ___ *Dining In–Philadelphia* | *8.95* | ___ *Dining In–Seattle, Vol. III* | *8.95* |
| ___ *Dining In–Phoenix* | *8.95* | ___ *Dining In–Washington, D.C.* | *8.95* |

☐ CHECK HERE IF YOU WOULD LIKE TO HAVE A
DIFFERENT DINING IN–COOKBOOK SENT TO YOU
ONCE A MONTH

Payable by MasterCard, Visa, or C.O.D. Returnable if not satisfied.
*List price plus $1.00 postage and handling for each book.*

**BILL TO:**

Name _____

Address _____

City _____ State ___ Zip _____

**SHIP TO:**

Name _____

Address _____

City _____ State ___ Zip _____

☐ Payment enclosed   ☐ Send C.O.D.   ☐ Charge

Visa # _____ Exp. Date _____

MasterCard # _____ Exp. Date _____

Signature _____

## PEANUT BUTTER PUBLISHING
2445 76th Avenue S.E. • Mercer Island, WA 98040
(206) 236-1982